SCHOLASTIC

MW00615645

Social & Emotional Learning

Essential Lessons for Student Success

Engaging Lessons, Strategies, and Tips
That Help Students Develop Self-Awareness
and Manage Social Challenges
So They Can Focus on Academics

Tom Conklin

New York · Toronto · London · Auckland · Sydney
Mexico City · New Delhi · Hong Kong · Buenos Aires

Teaching *Resources*

This book is dedicated to all of the amazing kids
I had the honor to work with at Bayside and the Homestead.

Acknowledgments

I thank all of my colleagues at Ocean Mental Health Services, in particular Teri Broo and Michelle Juska, for their help and encouragement as I developed much of the material in this book. I'd also like to thank Dr. Anthony Tasso for sharing his insights on psychological assessments, and Dr. Lona Whitmarsh for providing excellent clinical supervision and advice.

Finally, I must thank Dolores and Marcela for all of their incredible support—social and emotional.

Credits

Page 65: Diagnostic language for the three disorders is from the *Diagnostic and Statistical Manual of Disorders (5th ed.)*, published by the American Psychiatric Association (2013).

Page 123: Worksheet 23 adapts into teen-friendly language common "cognitive distortions" used by therapists. The original distortions were published in *Feeling Good* by David D. Burns, published by HarperCollins (1980).

Page 124: Worksheet 24 adapts a very common cognitive-behavioral therapy technique; in particular, from material in *A Guide to Rational Living* by Albert Ellis and Robert A. Harper, published by the Institute for Rational Living/Wilshire Book Company. Copyright © 1997 by the Albert Ellis Institute.

Every effort has been made to secure permission for the use of all copyrighted material. The publisher will gladly make any necessary corrections in future printings.

Edited by Mela Ottaiano
Cover design by Jorge J. Namerow
Interior design by Melinda Belter
Cover illustration by Lindsey Dekker
ISBN: 978-0-545-46529-8
Copyright © 2014 by Tom Conklin
All rights reserved.
Published by Scholastic Inc.
Printed in the U.S.A.

7 8 9 10   40   21 20

Contents

Introduction

Social and emotional learning (SEL) is an education reform whose time has come. It's based on a fairly simple idea: Students who are better able to understand and manage their own emotions while interacting constructively with others will be better learners. SEL began as a movement in the 1980s, and gained momentum in the 1990s with the publication of Daniel Goleman's best seller, *Emotional Intelligence: Why It Can Matter More Than IQ*. Today, all 50 states have SEL learning standards at the early childhood level. At the K–12 level, the Common Core State Standards (CCSS) contain standards reflecting the key SEL competencies of speaking and listening, cooperation skills, and problem-solving. Many states have adopted or are considering SEL standards for K–12.

Now, some educators might hear about the growth of SEL and think, "Oh, great. Another fad they're trying to shove into the curriculum! I can barely cover what I need to cover as is."

But not you.

You recognize that it's challenging enough to get through the curriculum without your progress being stunted by classroom management issues like poor behavior and student distractibility. You realize that the roots of classroom management issues lie in students' difficulty in managing emotions and social relationships, and that this has a direct and profound impact on their academic achievement. You understand that SEL isn't a bothersome addition to a teacher's workload, it's a necessary dimension in providing a quality education to all students.

If your gut instinct tells you that socially and emotionally competent students are better learners, here's a fact to back you up: A recent study involving over 270,000 K–12 students found that those who had participated in universal SEL programs had "significantly improved social and emotional skills, attitudes, behavior, and academic performance that reflected an 11-percentile-point gain in achievement" (Durlak, Weissberg, Dymnicki, Taylor, and Schellinger, 2011).

Yes, you read that correctly. *The study found that SEL boosted achievement scores by 11 points.*

But there is far more to SEL than the promise of higher test scores. A recent 50-year longitudinal study found that children who acquire SEL skills, such as self-awareness, restraint, and persistence, enjoyed more success in their lives. Similar studies link SEL skills to reduced mental health issues throughout life, stronger marriages, and improved physical health (Kahn, 2013). SEL skills, acquired in school, can yield lifetime benefits.

Of course, the eye-popping achievement results mentioned above were gained in schools with universal, comprehensive SEL programs—an approach that's beyond the scope of a stand-alone book. Think of this book as a beginning step in making SEL instruction a larger piece of your students' education. First, it gives an explanation of the importance of SEL as it pertains to the unique developmental challenges facing middle school students. That knowledge can help you advocate for SEL as a core element of all instruction in your school. These pages also share some of the basic social science theory that underlies the precepts of SEL. Finally, the book provides a variety of lesson plans covering fundamental SEL objectives that you can use to enhance your existing curriculum.

One final word before we begin our exploration of SEL and the middle school classroom. If you are at all intimidated by the prospect of incorporating social and emotional themes into your students' academic work, remember this—*you are already doing it.*

If you study literature and analyze characters' motives, actions, and relationships, you have an SEL classroom.

If you ever discuss current events, pop culture, or the arts and challenge students to think critically about the media they consume, you have an SEL classroom.

If you encourage your students to collaborate, cooperate, and communicate, you have an SEL classroom.

If you're a skilled and dedicated educator, then you already have an SEL classroom. Your SEL classroom will help your students become the best people they can be.

Using This Book

While SEL should be an essential core element of middle school education, the lessons and activities in this book are intended to enrich an existing language arts curriculum. You'll also find introductions to basic SEL concepts and their underlying theories, which can help you weave SEL into your instruction throughout the school year.

- The book opens with a unit on self, which explores basic dimensions of intrapersonal awareness.

- The next unit focuses on students' key interpersonal relationships.

- Finally, the book looks at common social and emotional challenges, as well as students' remarkable resilience.

The approach I take is far from a lock-step, scripted curriculum. Feel free to pick and choose and use the lessons as you see fit. However, you should know that self-awareness underlies all of the relationship-oriented material that comes after the first unit. It's advisable to start with a look at the material in the first section before exploring the subsequent units.

Refer back to the annotated table of contents, which presents each unit, the topics it covers, and the lessons included under each topic. The table of contents also identifies relevant academic skills exercised in each lesson.

SEL Objectives

The Collaborative for Academic, Social, and Emotional Learning (CASEL) is at the forefront of the SEL movement. Their website, www.casel.org, is a treasure trove of information on SEL, including current research on instruction and results, thorough evaluations of existing SEL curricula, and up-to-date information on SEL reforms in each state. CASEL has also identified a core set of skills that any SEL curriculum should address. I've adapted these skills into a set of numbered SEL learning objectives, presented in the chart below. To see how the lessons in this book have been correlated to the relevant CASEL skills, look for the "SEL Objectives" numbers listed with each lesson, and refer back to this chart to see details of those objectives.

Self-Awareness: The ability to recognize one's emotions and thoughts and their influence on behavior.

> 1. Accurately assessing one's strengths and limitations.
>
> 2. Possessing a well-grounded sense of confidence and optimism.

Self-Management: The ability to regulate one's emotions, thoughts, and behaviors in different situations.

> 3. Managing stress.
>
> 4. Motivating oneself.
>
> 5. Controlling impulses.
>
> 6. Setting and working toward achieving personal and academic goals.

Social Awareness: The ability to take the perspective of and empathize with others from diverse backgrounds and cultures.

> 7. To understand social and ethical norms of behavior.
>
> 8. Recognize family, school, and community resources and supports.

Relationship Skills: The ability to establish and maintain healthy and rewarding relationships with diverse individuals and groups.

> 9. Communicating clearly.
>
> 10. Listening actively.
>
> 11. Cooperating.
>
> 12. Resisting inappropriate social pressure.
>
> 13. Negotiating conflict constructively.
>
> 14. Seeking and offering help when needed.

Responsible Decision-Making: The ability to make constructive and respectful choices about personal behavior and social interactions.

> 15. Recognizing ethical standards, safety concerns, social norms.
>
> 16. Realistically evaluating consequences of various actions.
>
> 17. Considering well-being of self and others.

UNIT 1
Self

"WAS I THE SAME WHEN I GOT UP THIS MORNING? I ALMOST THINK I CAN REMEMBER
FEELING A LITTLE DIFFERENT. BUT IF I'M NOT THE SAME, THE NEXT QUESTION IS, WHO
IN THE WORLD AM I? AH, THAT'S THE GREAT PUZZLE!"

FROM *ALICE IN WONDERLAND*, BY LEWIS CARROLL

The voyage to self-discovery is one of the great themes of literature. This is especially true of young adult literature, whose readers have reached the age at which they leave behind the certainties of childhood and face the daunting prospect of adulthood. The eternal puzzle of youthful self-discovery, framed so memorably in Lewis Carroll's masterpieces about Alice and her mad adventures in Wonderland, raises a fundamental question:

How do we know ourselves?

Self-awareness is a challenge that has engaged history's greatest philosophers and literature's deepest characters—think of Hamlet wrestling with existential angst, or a Jane Austen heroine struggling to be herself in a rigidly conformist society. Besides being an eternal theme in literature, self-awareness is also a cornerstone concept in social and emotional learning. With true self-awareness comes self-acceptance and the ability to interact with others in constructive and fulfilling ways. It entails recognizing our emotions and developing the ability to manage those emotions constructively. Self-awareness also reflects a true grasp of our strengths, along with an understanding of one's personal traits and those traits we share with others. Without self-awareness, it's difficult to live a fulfilling, socially connected life.

So, when do we first begin to solidify that enduring sense of who we are, what we feel, and what we can be? At what age do we humans begin to form our identity? The middle school years.

Middle school coincides with the onset of puberty, and we are all familiar with what that means for the young people we encounter every day. The outward and obvious physical changes of puberty are accompanied by equally tumultuous psychological changes—we've all endured a teen's brooding self-absorption, his abrupt and puzzling mood swings, and his intense, passionate likes and dislikes. If the end result of the physical changes endured in puberty is a healthy adult body, the end result of the psychological changes will be a healthy adult identity.

The renowned psychologist Erik Erikson theorized that human development takes place as a series of psychosocial conflicts commonly experienced across the lifespan (Erikson, 1959, 1980, pp. 51–107). (See the chart on the next page.) According to Erikson, optimal human development requires the successful resolution of each developmental conflict. The conflict, which Erikson suggests lies at the center of adolescence, is *identity versus identity diffusion*.

Resolving the conflict between identity and identity diffusion, as described by Erikson, is core to healthy social and emotional functioning. Left unresolved, this conflict can lead to a lifetime of unsatisfactory relationships and a lack of self-fulfillment. People with a fully formed identity combine self-awareness with self-acceptance. A diffuse identity, on the other hand, may lead to an ever-shifting array of possible selves, and a persistent dissatisfaction with oneself and one's relationships. We see this unstable sense of self expressed by young teens in superficial ways, such as extreme hair styles, outrageous fashions, and pop culture obsessions. Identity diffusion can also lead teens to attempt to lose themselves in a pre-made identity through association with an existing clique or organization.

There are many ways that middle school educators can help students develop healthy self-awareness and acquire tools to avoid the enduring maze of identity diffusion. What follows are lessons that explore various aspects of identity from the middle school perspective in order to help young teens develop self-awareness.

Erik Erikson

A true giant of twentieth-century thought, Erik Erikson accomplished groundbreaking work in identity and developmental psychology. Here are Erikson's Psychosocial Stages.

STAGE/CRISIS	AGE	PSYCHOSOCIAL MODALITY
Trust vs. Mistrust	Infancy	To get To give in return
Autonomy vs. Shame and Doubt	Toddlerhood (ages 1 ½ to 3 years)	To hold on To let go
Initiative vs. Guilt	Preschool (3 to 5 years)	To make (to try things) To "make like" (playing)
Industry vs. Inferiority	Elementary school (6 years to puberty)	To make things To make things together
Identity vs. Identity Diffusion	Adolescence (puberty to 20 years)	To be oneself (or not to be) To share being oneself
Intimacy vs. Isolation	Early adulthood (20s and 30s)	To lose and find oneself in another
Generativity vs. Stagnation	Middle age (40s and 50s)	To make be To take care of
Integrity vs. Despair	Late adulthood (60s and older)	To be, through having been To face not being

(Erikson, 1959, 1980, p. 178)

Self-Awareness

As children enter the teen years, their self-awareness changes significantly (Santrock, 2012). Younger children tend to have a rigidly consistent sense of self, mainly consisting of concrete attributes. *("I'm right-handed. I'm good at math. I love Minecraft.")* By the time he is a teen, a child's self-awareness will reflect a developing capacity for abstract thinking, along with a growing sense of independence. This allows for contradictions in the teen's sense of self. For instance, by the time she hits the middle school years, a teen will be aware that she is apt to behave one way at home with her parents and siblings, and quite a different way when hanging out with friends at school.

Another significant development in middle school is that teens are all too likely to become obsessed with the topic of "me." (I'll never forget the time I ran a group on "Interpersonal Relationships" in which a 14-year-old girl spent the entire session gazing at her own reflection in a compact mirror.) Teen egocentrism does not necessarily lead to narcissism—it can lead to painful self-consciousness and harsh self-criticism. As we'll see, adolescence is the stage at which we develop the tendency for idealized thinking, and this tendency affects self-conception. The gap between a teen's "ideal self" and what they perceive to be their actual self can be the source of a lot of angst. Research suggests that a way to help young teens construct a healthy self-concept is to challenge them to consider all of their *possible selves* (Markus & Nurius, 1986). By considering their potential for future development, teens "reframe" the gap between ideal/actual selves from a description of present failure to motivation for positive change.

Often, middle schoolers will have a powerful sense of their selves—their wants and needs, likes and dislikes—without applying any kind of critical thinking to their self-assessments. This simple activity uses an adolescent's natural self-absorption as the inspiration to begin the process of self-awareness. It allows students to brainstorm all of the things that make them who they are, while asking them to express their qualities in appropriate, descriptive ways.

LESSON 1

All About Me

SEL Objectives: 1, 9, 10

Preparing for the Lesson

This activity is a good icebreaker to use in the early days of a school year.

Warm Up

Tell students that they are about to do an activity that will help them get to know each other better. Ask, "Who are you?" and allow students to brainstorm things that describe them as individuals. Encourage them to be as descriptive as possible, including traits that go deeper than mere physical descriptions. Ask leading questions to help them begin to think more critically and abstractly about themselves:

- What things make you one of a kind?

- What things do you have in common with your family? Your friends?

- What things about you have been true since you were born? What things about you have changed, or might change?

Using the Lesson

1. At the top of a blank sheet of paper have students write their name and the title "All About Me." (Or have them use the opening pages of their journals, if they are keeping journals.)

2. Instruct students to come up with words that describe who they are. Challenge them to sort their self-descriptive words into organized lists. (Note that advanced students can write their descriptions in essay form.)

3. Here are some suggested ways students may organize their lists. Choose the method that is most appropriate for your students, depending on their skills level or the demands of your curriculum.

   ### BASIC LEVEL: NOUNS, ADJECTIVES, VERBS

   Have students sort their lists according to parts of speech:

   Nouns: words that name concrete facts about the students, such as their gender, relationships (*son* or *daughter*, *brother* or *sister*), ethnic identity, grade level, and so on.

   Descriptive words: adjectives that describe each individual's qualities, both concrete (*tall, short, athletic*) and more abstract (*happy, funny, eager, shy, smart*).

   Verbs: words that describe what they do each day (*read, play games, talk/text, study, practice piano*).

INTERMEDIATE LEVEL: FACT AND OPINION

Take a more critical-thinking approach by having students sort their list into two columns: "Fact" and "Opinion."

Fact: aspects of the student that are objectively true (such as gender, age, grade level, family role).

Opinion: aspects of the student that are either personal tastes or subjective self-assessments (such as, "I'm funny," "I'm going to be famous," "I'm shy").

Allow students to share their self-descriptors, without saying which of the two lists each descriptor is on, then ask peers if each one is fact or opinion. Expect some lively discussions as one teen's "fact" will be called "opinion" by peers ("Are you *really* going to be famous?"). Explaining and justifying self-perceptions can be a positive step in developing students' self-awareness.

ADVANCED LEVEL: AUTOBIOGRAPHY

Students can use a separate sheet of paper to write a brief autobiographical essay. Explain to students that their essay should contain all of the essential facts of their lives (such as birthdate, family history, where they have lived and so on). The essay should also contain information that conveys to the reader what kind of person the student is. Students should mention their abstract, intangible qualities, such as their moods, how they get along with others, and their personal strengths.

Wrap Up

After students share their worksheet or essay with their peers, go around the class and ask volunteers to name one thing they have learned about a classmate. You can also ask them to state something they might have learned about themselves during the process.

Extending the Lesson

This activity offers a great opportunity for students to consider how others see them, as well as how they have grown and changed over time. After they have discussed their All About Me descriptions, ask them the following questions:

- How might a parent describe you?

- What would a sibling add to the description?

- How would the description be different if it had been completed by your former kindergarten teacher?

Social & Emotional Learning © 2014 by Tom Conklin, Scholastic Teaching Resources

Personality Traits

Personality. We often use the word in a general sense to indicate the basic impression that an individual will have on other people. ("Oh, she has a great personality!") To a psychologist, however, *personality* specifically refers to the enduring characteristics of individuals over their lifespan (Santrock, 2012). A common way of conceptualizing the enduring characteristics of personality is through trait theory.

Language arts instructors are, of course, familiar with the trait theory of good writing. Just as writing can be broken down into traits such as voice, ideas, organization, and so on, many psychologists believe that personality can be analyzed as a set of broad and enduring traits, and that these traits can be identified and measured using psychological tests.

A prevalent trait theory of personality is the so-called "Big Five Factors of Personality" model (Santrock, 2012). Developed in the 1960s, the Big Five model suggests that human personality is expressed by a set of five stable and enduring "supertraits." Each of these supertraits covers more narrow personality traits. This chart presents the Big Five supertraits and their subset traits.

Openness	Conscientiousness	Extraversion	Agreeableness	Neuroticism
Imaginative or practical	Organized or disorganized	Sociable or retiring	Softhearted or ruthless	Calm or anxious
Interested in variety or routine	Careful or careless	Fun-loving or somber	Trusting or suspicious	Secure or insecure
Independent or conforming	Disciplined or impulsive	Affectionate or reserved	Helpful or uncooperative	Self-satisfied or self-pitying

(Santrock, 2012, p. 359)

Identifying personality traits can be a powerful tool in raising a young teen's self-awareness, and it's something adolescents often take to naturally. Why? Many are already thoroughly schooled in the trait model of personality because of the video games they play.

Many video games popular with middle schoolers have players create characters and set them loose in artificial worlds. (*Sims* is probably the most popular example of this genre.) As they create their characters, players are able to choose a set of core personality traits from a long list of options. The traits that a young player may choose for his or her virtual self says a lot about that player—not necessarily about the traits the player already may possess in reality, but about what the player might aspire to become. The following activity uses a creative trait model as a way to develop your students' understanding of who they are and what they might one day be.

LESSON 2

What Are My Traits?

SEL Objectives: 1

Preparing for the Lesson
Make copies of Worksheet 1: What Are My Traits? (page 99).

Warm Up
Ask students if they have ever played a computer game that allows them to create their own character. Have students familiar with the process describe how they go about creating a character. Ask students familiar with the games to describe what traits are and how they pick traits for their alter-ego characters in the game.

Using the Lesson
1. Distribute the worksheet to the class. Explain that these are traits you might use to create a character for a virtual reality computer game.

2. Have students review the list of traits on the worksheet and discuss among themselves any questions they may have regarding the traits. Let students define the traits in their own words.

3. Have students go through the list of traits and mark those traits they already possess, along with those they hope to develop in the future.

4. After students have marked their traits, lead a class discussion on their work. Talk about the fact that some traits are "hardwired" at birth (such as shy or excitable) and others are things you consciously choose to be (such as vegetarian or eco-friendly). Other traits come about by working to develop "hardwired" traits for a purpose. (For instance, if a student is hardwired to be friendly, then he or she can work to fine-tune that trait into being a "schmoozer," a "social butterfly," or a "born salesperson," depending on his or her wishes.)

Social & Emotional Learning © 2014 by Tom Conklin, Scholastic Teaching Resources

5. Have students explain why they wish to develop their future traits—for instance, whether those traits will help them accomplish life goals or be happy. Also discuss how they can harness traits that might land them into trouble (rebellious) and turn them into something positive (adventurous). Talk about how traits are not necessarily good or bad, but how we use them in our relationships with other people can have positive or negative results.

Wrap Up

Have students quickly go through the list and identify traits that they look for in a friend. Also have them discuss which traits they already possess that are attractive to other people, and why.

Extending the Lesson

Challenge students to write a short story featuring their "trait self," as identified on the worksheet, as the main character. Have them develop a plot and actions that allows their "trait self" to demonstrate their various traits. Encourage students to *show* the traits, not *tell* the reader that their character possesses the traits. Have students exchange stories and see if they can identify the different traits that each of their characters are meant to be demonstrating.

Introversion/Extraversion and Optimism/Pessimism

Two sets of traits that are core to personality—and that are grasped intuitively by young teenagers—are optimism/pessimism and introversion/extraversion. Unlike traits whose expression are affected by a social context, these innate traits affect how we *respond* to social situations. First, let's look at introversion/extraversion.

The terms *introvert* and *extravert* were popularized by the brilliant Swiss psychologist Carl Jung in his landmark book *Psychological Types*. According to Jung, extraversion and introversion are general attitudes that color an individual's functioning in the domains of thinking, feeling, sensation, and intuition. The extravert is externally motivated and, in social situations, has a need "to join in and get 'with it.'" Jung describes the extravert as a classic people-person, interested in making new friends and not being too choosy in doing so, with "a strong tendency to make a show of oneself." The introvert, on the other hand, prefers to maintain a smaller circle of friends. According to Jung, the introvert "holds aloof . . . does not join in . . . in a large gathering he feels lonely and lost" (Jung, 1936, pp. 140–141).

When thinking of young teenagers in the context of introversion and extraversion, it's important to keep in mind that these are not hard-and-fast categories. Like most psychological traits, introversion and extraversion exist along a continuum, with most people somewhere in the middle, far from the most extreme poles. In 1927, social scientist Kimball Young coined the term "ambivert" to describe those of us with a personality type between introvert and extravert. Most middle schoolers will land closer to "ambivert" than pure introvert or extravert.

It's also important to understand that introversion and extraversion are not synonymous with character traits like shyness or aggression. In her recent bestseller, *Quiet: The Power of Introverts in a World That Can't Stop Talking*, Susan Cain defines the two personality traits according to how each is "energized." According to Cain, extraverts are energized by being with other people, while introverts draw energy from within themselves and find that other people drain their energy (Cain, 2012).

Clearly, middle school is a critical period for students as they transition from the academic and social fundamentals of grade school to more challenging and abstract work. This is the time when you might see introverts start to shine academically, and more extraverted students begin to struggle. Keep this in mind when making assignments, and consider pairing introverts and extraverts for team collaborations. (Worksheet 2 provides a simple tool to identify introverts and extraverts in your classes.)

Regardless of whether they fall closer to the introverted or extraverted end of the scale, it's important that teens understand the positive qualities of their type and not embrace negative stereotypes associated with it. Introverted teens may internalize the negative labels of "wallflower" or "nerd." And some young teens—especially boys—may own the labels "attention-seeker" or "hyper," when in truth they are extraverts who derive more energy from larger and more fast-paced social settings. Remember, middle schoolers are just entering the stage of life at which they will form an enduring identity. The challenge is to help teens embrace the positive aspects of their personality type and harness their energies in the most socially beneficial way.

INTROVERTS VS. EXTRAVERTS—WHO MAKES THE GRADE?

Which student enjoys more success in the classroom—the quiet kid who keeps to himself, or the outgoing chatterbox and team player? It depends, to a large part, on what grade they are in.

A team of psychologists in the U.K. conducted a study that correlated students' school performance to various personality traits, including extraversion and introversion. They found that extraverts outperform introverts during the grade school years, but that introverts generally have stronger grades in secondary school. Why the switch? "Introverts may have an advantage over extraverts with respect to the ability to consolidate learning, as well as lower distractibility and better study habits," the authors concluded (Furnham, Chamorro-Premuzic, and McDougall, 2003).

Half Empty or Half Full?

Ask just about any seventh grader, "Are you Eeyore or Tigger? Donkey or Shrek?" and they immediately understand what you are asking—are you upbeat and look on the bright side? Or do you tend to be gloomy, and always see what's wrong with things? In short, are you an optimist or a pessimist?

Like introversion/extraversion, the traits of optimism and pessimism are expressed through our social interactions. But unlike the more benign introversion/extraversion spectrum, excesses of pessimism are linked to psychological disorders, such as depression, as well as to risky behaviors. In one discussion of the topic I was leading with a group of teens, a girl admitted that she was usually a "Shrek," but that she would use drugs and alcohol in order to make herself more "Donkey"—carefree, fun-loving, and (so she thought) popular.

Martin Seligman, founder of the positive psychology movement, has done extensive research on optimism, pessimism, and their links to social and emotional functioning, especially among children and teens. According to Seligman, optimism and pessimism run deeper than simple "positive thinking" and "negative thinking"—they are, in fact, styles of

critical thinking (Seligman, 1995). According to Seligman, optimists and pessimists have different ways of analyzing events and their causes. These different habits of thought result in what he calls different "explanatory styles." When analyzing any negative experience, children and teens will consider its causes along three dimensions: permanence, pervasiveness, and personal.

PERMANENCE: Are the causes of bad events temporary or permanent?

PERVASIVENESS: Do bad things occur in certain areas of life, or do they follow you around like a black cloud?

PERSONAL: Are you personally to blame for the bad things that happen in your life? (Seligman, 1995)

The child's customary response to these questions will determine whether she is an optimist or pessimist.

What's more, to a greater extent than extraversion/introversion, optimism and pessimism are learned responses. Seligman coined the term "learned helplessness" to describe individuals whose environments have caused them to internalize the belief that negative things are permanent, pervasive, and personal. These individuals are at higher risk for depression, anxiety, and other mental health disorders. See the Stress section in Unit 3 for some detailed suggestions on helping the Shreks and Eeyores in your class to cope with the "dark clouds" in their lives.

For our purposes here—to cultivate self-awareness—use the simple self-assessments that follow in order to allow your students to determine their temperaments regarding introversion/extraversion and optimism/pessimism. Bear in mind that these are not scientific personality tests, but they can give you and your students some insight on how they relate to other people, and whether they see the glass of life as half full or half empty.

LESSON 3

What's My Attitude?

SEL Objectives: 1, 2, 11

Preparing for the Lesson

Make copies of Worksheet 2: Introvert or Extravert (page 100) and Worksheet 3: Optimist or Pessimist (page 101). If you choose to extend the lesson by making a class bulletin board, as suggested in Extending the Lesson, gather the materials you will need for the board.

- Worksheet 2 is adapted from a free on-line self-assessment from author Susan Cain's website. The original can be found at: http://www.thepowerofintroverts.com/2011/01/27/quiz-are-you-an-introvert-or-an-extrovert-and-why-does-it-matter/

- Worksheet 3 is adapted from a well-known free optimism/pessimism quiz, the LOT-R, found at: http://www.psy.miami.edu/faculty/ccarver/CCscales.html

Warm Up

Ask students what it means to have an attitude. Discuss what the word *attitude* means. Students will probably think of it terms of "good attitude" or "bad attitude." Share with them this definition of *attitude:* it's your "readiness to act or react in a certain way." (This is Jung's definition of *attitude* from his *Psychological Types* [Jung, 1923].) Have students discuss their own attitudes, that is, how they tend to act and react in different situations (say, school and home). Does their attitude change much from situation to situation? What about their attitude is fairly consistent?

Using the Lesson

1. Distribute Worksheets 2 and 3 and have students complete them. They should work in small teams so they can collaborate to work out how to score the sheets. (Some students may have difficulty grasping that their final score may be a negative number. In my experience, more mathematically able students are best able to explain it to peers.)

2. After students have finished the worksheets, discuss the results. Deepen the discussion with the following questions:

   - Are you mainly an optimist? A pessimist? What does it mean to have those attitudes?

   - Suppose you have a big test in two weeks. How does an optimist prepare? How does a pessimist? (Some students might say that an optimist thinks he doesn't need to study. Others will say that a pessimist will think he is bound to fail, so there is no point to studying.) If you do study, will you be more optimistic or pessimistic as you take the test?

   - Who is an introvert? Who is an extravert? What does it mean to have those attitudes?

   - What are the strengths of introverts? What are the strengths of extraverts?

   - Can you change your attitude if you are introvert or extravert? If so, how?

Wrap Up

Write the word *ambivert* on the board and explain that it's a word used to describe people who are outgoing sometimes and introverted at other times. Challenge students to coin a word of their own to describe people who are sometimes optimistic and sometimes pessimistic.

Extending the Lesson

This activity, by making you and your students aware of their social attitudes, can be a tool for classroom management. I have designed the scoring to use scales from –10 to +10 so that the results can be displayed on an X, Y graph. This lets you and your students easily see where they fall on an "Attitude Latitude" scale.

Draw a simple X, Y graph on the board or, if appropriate for your grade levels, make a bulletin board onto which your students can place themselves based on their scores. Introversion/Extraversion should be along the X (horizontal) axis, with values from –10 to +10. Optimism/Pessimism should be laid out similarly along the Y (vertical) axis. Students will then be placed in the appropriate quadrant, depending on their scores. Here's how the graph should be laid out:

What's Your Attitude Latitude?

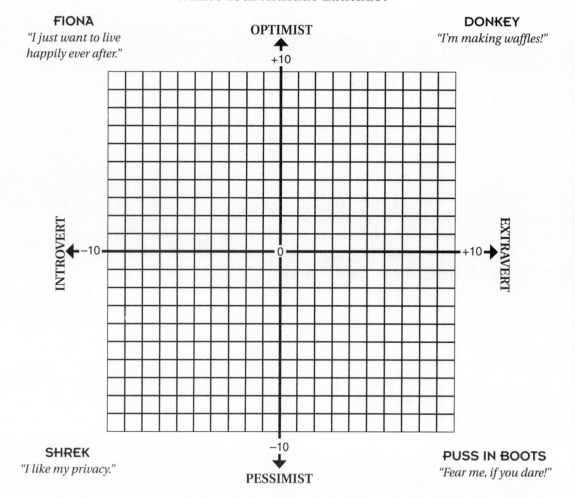

FIONA
"I just want to live happily ever after."

OPTIMIST +10

DONKEY
"I'm making waffles!"

INTROVERT −10   0   +10 **EXTRAVERT**

SHREK
"I like my privacy."

−10
PESSIMIST

PUSS IN BOOTS
"Fear me, if you dare!"

TIP For added support, you might use fictional characters to symbolize each of the four "attitude latitudes." I've used characters from the movie *Shrek*. (You can pick others that your students might find appealing from other sources, such as the Harry Potter or Hunger Games series.) On my graph, a student who scored -4 on Worksheet 2 and +3 on Worksheet 3 would be placed near the middle of the "Fiona" quadrant.

Once the graph is complete, students will see how they relate to each other according to their optimism/pessimism and introversion/extraversion traits. Use this information when having students work in teams throughout the school year—you might not want your "Donkeys" teaming up all of the time, and you should be aware that some "Shreks" will need to be prodded into working with their more outgoing peers. Collaborating with fellow students who do not share their attitudes offers young teens great opportunities to develop their social skills.

Social & Emotional Learning © 2014 by Tom Conklin, Scholastic Teaching Resources

Self-Esteem

Few topics that fall under the heading of social and emotional learning have been as thoroughly researched as self-esteem. Almost everyone is familiar with the facts: high self-esteem is a predictor of success in school, while low self-esteem sets a student up to fail. The key to boosting self-esteem is to have young people focus on appreciating themselves, which in practice means encouraging them to internalize and repeat positive and self-supporting messages.

Well, not so fast.

While some educators accept some or all of these ideas about self-esteem, the above "facts" are poorly supported by research. Indeed, many "facts" about self-esteem appear to be self-perpetuating myths. This is not to suggest that healthy, positive self-esteem doesn't matter in a teen's life. It does mean that it's vital for educators to understand the actual role self-esteem plays in a teen's social and emotional functioning and to help teens construct authentic, positive self-esteem instead of simply attempting to force-feed them good feelings about themselves.

Most of the social science research on self-esteem leads to the conclusion that positive self-esteem is not the *cause* of success in school and other areas of life that matter to teens, it's the *product* of such success. An exhaustive meta-analysis of the research literature on self-esteem found that study after study demonstrated only modest correlation between school success and self-esteem, with little evidence that high self-esteem actually causes success. In fact, the authors suggest that artificially inflated self-esteem has a mild negative effect on student performance, by providing positive feedback that is unearned by actual success (Baumeister, Campbell, Krueger, and Vohs, 2003).

You might assume that Martin Seligman, founder of the positive psychology movement, would be a powerful advocate for self-esteem education. He is, instead, one of its harshest critics. There is, Seligman claims, no effective way to teach "feeling good" that does not first teach "doing well":

"Feelings of self-esteem in particular, and happiness in general, develop as side effects—of mastering challenges, working successfully, overcoming frustration and boredom, and winning. The feeling of self-esteem is a byproduct of doing well" (Seligman, 1995, p. 32).

Seligman goes on to suggest that programs designed to explicitly boost children's self-esteem have instead contributed to a contrary phenomenon—an increase in childhood and adolescent depression. Speaking from my own clinical experience, there is not much that can more thoroughly darken the mood of a teen wrestling with depression than explicitly discussing her self-esteem. On the other hand, successfully competing in word games, solving brain teasers, writing a well-constructed and honest poem—these and other opportunities to demonstrate skill can help lift the spirits of kids with depressed moods. This is why many experts in social and emotional learning refer not to self-esteem, but self-efficacy, which is "the belief that one has mastery over the events of one's life and can meet challenges as they come up" (Goleman, 1995, p. 89). Albert Bandura, a leading researcher of the topic of self-efficacy, says that people who have developed it "bounce back from failures; they approach things in terms of how to handle them rather than worrying about what can go wrong" (Goleman, 1995, p. 90).

(See Unit 3 for more on the topic of resiliency.)

Emotions

Ask anyone to define the word *emotion*. The answer you get will depend on whom you ask: a poet might say emotions are the feelings that well up inside of you as you experience a glorious sunset or hear a baby's laugh; a neuroscientist would explain that emotion is the product of a complex set of signals sent between neurons in the brain's limbic system and prefrontal cortex in response to a stimulus.

For our purposes, let's start with a basic definition of emotion popular with psychologists today: "Emotion is a feeling, or affect, that occurs when a person is engaged in an action that is important to him or her, especially to his or her well-being" (Santrock, 2012, p. 301). Emotions are expressed through behaviors that show whether the individual finds the emotions to be pleasant or unpleasant, and their intensity can vary greatly. Finally, emotions arise in a social environment and are the result of our interactions with other people.

Young teens feel emotions more intensely than do adults. A study of middle school students and their parents found that the kids were, at any given moment, five times more likely to report being very happy, and three times more likely to feel very unhappy, than were their parents (Larson & Richards, 1994). Those powerful adolescent emotions are the result of surging hormones and a limbic system (the region of the brain that generates emotion) that is developing more rapidly than the prefrontal cortex (the brain region that regulates emotions). Environmental and social pressures also add to the swirl of joy, rage, embarrassment, and crushing boredom that can make up a middle schooler's daily emotional roller coaster. It might be because young adolescents feel their emotions so intensely that they often deny that the emotions exist or have any sway over their thinking and behavior. Helping the young teen develop the cognitive skills to recognize and parse emotions as accurately as possible is a first step in developing his emotional management skills.

Psychologists use a variety of models to describe emotions. A common model sorts emotions into two broad categories: basic emotions and self-conscious emotions. *Basic emotions* include surprise, joy, anger, sadness, fear, and disgust and are present in both humans and animals. These develop and are first expressed during infancy. *Self-conscious emotions* develop during toddlerhood, as the growing child develops a cognitive sense of herself as an autonomous being. Self-conscious emotions include jealousy, empathy, and embarrassment (Santrock, 2012, p. 304).

Another model of emotion, and one that middle school students intuitively grasp, is Robert Plutchik's structural model (Plutchik, 1991). According to Plutchik, emotions are like colors, in that there is a set of primary emotions that combine to create the rich variety of emotional experiences we all share.

In my experience, middle schoolers will describe their emotions in the most blunt terms—"good," "bad," "mad," "sad." Once they understand that their basic emotions can combine and lead to more complex emotions—like red and yellow combine to make orange—young teens begin to recognize and describe a far greater spectrum of emotion.

Another key concept regarding emotions is that they are expressed through behavior. Too often, middle schoolers (and the adults who work with them) will "chase behaviors" by reacting to provocations instead of trying to understand the emotions that motivate them. This can lead to self-perpetuating cycles of negative emotions and bad behavior. The Aggression section in Unit 3 (page 62) will go into more detail on anger management techniques. For now, here are two activities that will provide students with practice in more fundamental skills:

- Identifying emotions
- Expressing emotions

LESSON 4

Feelings

SEL Objectives: 1, 2, 16

Preparing for the Lesson
Make copies of Worksheet 4: Feelings (page 102).

> - Worksheet 4 is adapted from material in *The Emotions* by Robert Plutchik, published by University Press of America (1991).

Warm Up
Ask students if they know what makes up the different colors we see. If none of the students brings it up, point out that every color we see is some combination of primary colors.

Next, ask students to define *emotion*. They will probably define the word by giving examples of different emotions instead of focusing on a more general definition. Share with them a variation of the definition given earlier: "An emotion is what you feel when something that matters is happening to you." Brainstorm a list of emotions with students. Ask them to come up with different ways to sort them: positive and negative, strong and weak, and so on.

Tell students that you are going to explore how emotions are like colors.

Using the Lesson
1. Distribute the worksheet and review it with students. Tell students that the primary emotions at the top of the page combine to form the emotions listed below, just as primary colors blend to make all of the other colors.

2. Have volunteers pick one of the complex feelings listed and explain how the primary emotions "add up" to make the complex feeling. In each case, have the student identify a time in which she felt a complex feeling. Challenge her to identify

the primary emotions that "added up" to cause the complex feeling.

Examples:

- "It was before the standardized test. I *anticipated* that it would be hard, and I was *afraid* I would do poorly. That made me feel *anxiety*."

- "It was when I first held my puppy. I felt *joy*, and I also *trusted* that the dog would love me. That made me feel *love*, too."

- "It was when I saw my birthday presents. I *trusted* my family would get me something good, and I knew I would be *surprised* since I couldn't guess what the gifts were. That made me feel *curious*."

3. Have all the students complete the worksheet by writing a paragraph to explain how two primary emotions "added up" to a complex feeling.

 TIP Plutchik developed a colorful graphic to show how complex emotions interrelate. Search the Internet using the terms *Plutchik emotion wheel*. The Plutchik wheel is a fascinating way to present emotions, and middle-schoolers instantly "get it."

Wrap Up

Have students keep a "feelings diary." In it, they name one complex emotion that they feel over the course of a day and try to identify what caused it. Have them record where they felt the emotion, who was with them, and what was going on. Challenge them to describe how primary emotions "add up" to cause their feelings.

Extending the Lesson

Have students choose one (or more) of the complex emotions. Have them write a poem that will express how it feels to have that emotion—challenge them to not use the name of the emotion, or any of the primary emotions associated with it, in their poem.

Brainstorm with students the sorts of details they can use in their poems to convey the emotions. Use the following list for ideas.

Causes: What things happen to make you feel the emotion?

Sensations: What color does the emotion make you see? How does it taste? Smell? What sounds does it make you hear? What other metaphors can you use to make the reader feel your emotion? (Is it a storm? A cool breeze?)

Actions: What sorts of things do you do when you feel the emotion?

Reactions: How do other people act when they see you with the emotion? What emotions do your actions cause in them?

Aftermath: How do you feel once the emotion passes? What consequences are there for your actions while feeling the emotion?

 Social & Emotional Learning © 2014 by Tom Conklin, Scholastic Teaching Resources

Cognition

"INTELLIGENCE IS WHAT YOU USE WHEN YOU DON'T KNOW WHAT TO DO."

—JEAN PIAGET

Jean Piaget liked to think about thinking. A giant figure in education theory, the Swiss-born psychologist came up with a model of cognitive development that has been hugely influential for the past 60 years. Piaget's model suggests that each child constructs his or her own knowledge and understanding of the world and how it works. The essence of education, according to Piaget, is to guide a student's discovery of knowledge and not to simply drill facts and figures into the student's mind. Piaget's work has informed early childhood education for generations, and his constructivist approach has big implications for social and emotional education, especially in the middle school years.

According to Piaget's theory, as children grow, they pass through a series of six cognitive stages, from the sensorimotor reactions of a newborn infant to the capacity for abstract thought, which Piaget labeled the formal operational stage. In Piaget's model, the ability to reason abstractly, without reference to concrete models, develops when the child is between the ages of 11 and 15—in other words, during the middle school years.

The curriculum reflects this. The middle school years are the stage when a math student progresses from arithmetic to pre-algebra to solving algebraic equations. It's the stage when the language arts curriculum evolves from a focus on vocabulary and basic comprehension to more nuanced discussions of metaphor, characterization, and literary themes. It's not just homework that grows more complicated during the middle school years, of course! This is also the stage at which the young teen's social interactions grow increasingly complex, for a variety of reasons.

First, as he develops the capacity for abstract thought, a young teen's ability to assess other people's emotional states and motivations increases, a cognitive skill that psychologists call *perspective taking*. This growing awareness that other people have different viewpoints and feel their own emotions takes place, conversely, as the teen's own egocentrism is increasing. In addition, the teen's maturing body causes him to develop romantic interests, with all of the emotional volatility that this entails. The adolescent also begins to operate from a sense of idealism, and may constantly be comparing himself, his family, peers, and authority figures (such as teachers!) to his own idea of what those people ought to be. Heightened sensitivity, egocentrism, idealism, romantic desires, and more. It's not easy to be a middle schooler!

Fortunately, the teen's developing capacity for abstract thought is a tool for managing the welter of emotions she feels. Cognitive behavioral therapy (CBT) is a form of treatment that coaches people to consciously challenge the "automatic thoughts" that cause them to misinterpret or "over interpret" social cues, a habit that's the root cause of much emotional distress. The Stress section in Unit 3 goes into more detail on cognitive coping strategies. For now, let's focus on the implications of the thought-provoking quote from Piaget that opened this section: "Intelligence is what you use when you don't know what to do."

In his recent best-seller, *Thinking, Fast and Slow*, Nobel-prize winning psychologist Daniel Kahneman popularizes the notion that we all use two types of thinking, which he calls System 1 and System 2. System 1 is basically "autopilot" mode—it stands for our constant stream of impressions, intuitions, and intentions. System 2, on the other hand, is the type of thinking Piaget was talking about in the quote above, which demands effort and strict attention. From a middle school perspective, System 1 is a student's "gut instinct;" it is what she uses to quickly detect hostility in a voice or recognize a friend's face in a crowded lunchroom. System 2 kicks in when the same young teen puts her "thinking cap" on to analyze character motivations in *Romeo and Juliet* or to solve an equation (Kahneman, 2011).

If middle school is the stage when a student is able to focus her attention to solve an equation or analyze a story, it's also the stage at which she can begin to use her "slow thinking" skills to better manage her off-the-cuff, emotion-based responses to challenging social situations. The first step in helping a young teen to use her rapidly developing cognitive skills to manage her emotions is making the teen aware that a fast, instinctive, emotion-based response to a challenging situation is just that—a knee-jerk response that may or may not be based on an accurate reading of the situation.

For instance, picture an eighth grader who walks into the library, where a group of her peers are sitting at a table carrying on a lively conversation filled with laughter. As the girl approaches the table, the peers fall silent. The girl's System 1 instantly assumes that they were talking about her and stopped when she approached. This causes her a pang of embarrassment and anger, which might make her lash out at her peers, or cause her to slink away. She's apt to spend the next few hours allowing her System 2 to spin elaborate theories for this "snub" and nursing a sense of outraged self-pity in silent isolation.

Although her assumption of bad intent by her peers is just that, an assumption, a typical 13-year-old in this situation will be convinced that her gut-level reading of it is correct. This is why every anger-management course begins with the basic instruction to count to ten or take space when you feel provoked. It's to give System 2 a chance to analyze the situation and your possible responses before System 1 establishes an interpretation that is swift, emotion-based, and faulty. (See Unit 3 for more on teen anger and aggression.)

Of course, the concept of System 1 and System 2 thought is too abstract for typical middle schoolers to fully understand. They may intuitively grasp the concept, however, when they discuss in their own terms how they respond to provocations. One teen I worked with used the angel/devil metaphor to describe her ways of responding to provoking situations; she said she had a devil on one shoulder that was always looking for a fight, and an angel on the other shoulder that told her to calm down. The problem, according to the girl, is that the devil always shouted, while the angel could only whisper. Other metaphors you can use to describe the two systems in a way that teens understand are "hot thoughts/cool thoughts," or, as I prefer, Kahneman's metaphor of "fast thinking" and "slow thinking."

In the spirit of Piaget, I like to have the teens I work with actually experience the effects of System 1 and System 2 before discussing their "fast thoughts" and "slow thoughts." Below is one activity, Brain Freezers, that will provide your students with the chance to experience firsthand the two cognitive systems. These can lead to that "ah-ha!" moment when a teen understands the difference between swift, intuitive *reactions* and carefully considered *responses*.

LESSON 5

Brain Freezers

SEL Objectives: 1, 2, 5, 10

Preparing the Lesson
Make copies of Worksheet 5: Brain Freezers (page 103).

Warm Up
Invite students to share favorite riddles with each other. After they have posed a few riddles, ask students what makes a riddle fun. (Possible answers: When they're tricky. When the answers are a surprise. When they're funny.) Tell students they are going to tackle a page full of riddles and brainteasers.

Using the Lesson
1. Distribute Worksheet 5. Have students work individually or in small groups to answer all of the riddles on the worksheet. As they start, challenge them to answer each riddle as quickly as possible. You may want to give them a time limit to complete all eight, such as 10 or 15 minutes.

2. When students are done, ask them which riddles were hard and which were easy. Which ones took longer to solve? Students will probably say that riddles 1–4 (column 1) were easier and that they solved them more quickly.

TIP You may prefer to use riddles and brainteasers not as a one-time activity, but as a daily ritual. If so, reserve one corner of your board for your daily riddle. Label that corner "Brain Freezer," or whatever clever name for the challenge you choose. Each day, write a riddle or brainteaser in the corner, along with an offer for extra-credit points or some other reward. Rules for the challenge should remain constant:

- First correct response wins
- One guess per student
- The puzzle remains until someone answers it correctly

If you choose this option, use the riddles on the handout for your Brain Freezers as a start for this daily ritual. You can also search the Internet, using the terms *counterintuitive riddles* or *lateral thinking riddles*, for more riddles to use.

3. Then ask students to share their answers to all of the riddles, one riddle at a time, and write the most common answers on the board. (Expect that there will be a strong consensus of answers for riddles 1–4, and a wide variety of answers for riddles 5–8.) Then go over the correct answers, using these notes to explain them.

COLUMN 1

1. Answer: $5. Most students will quickly provide the intuitive answer: $10. But it's wrong. If the game cost $10, then the console cost $10 + $110, or $120. The correct response is $5 ($5 + $105 = $110). If your students got the wrong answer, tell them they are in good company. More than half the students at prestigious universities like Harvard, MIT, and Princeton come up with the same wrong answer (Kahneman, 2011, p. 45)!

2. Answer: 5 minutes. Most students will answer 100 minutes. Point out that the rate stays the same, regardless of the number of machines at work.

3. Answer: None, since Noah built the ark. Note: This riddle is so common in psychological studies that the effect it illustrates is called "The Moses Illusion" (Kahneman, 2011, p. 73).

4. Answer: The student's name. This is a variation of the Moses Illusion mentioned above, in which the context primes a quick response that happens to be wrong. Be prepared for an avalanche of "June" responses.

COLUMN 2

5. Answer: A chessboard. Unlike "Moses Illusion" riddles, students are challenged here to provide a context for the action. They will wrack their brains and usually guess "a fairy tale," or "Middle Earth," or some variation of a fantasy story. The actual solution is both simple and prosaic.

6. Answer: "Are you asleep yet?" Students will attack this challenge, assuming that there are any number of possible answers. There are not, and you will probably get a wide variety of unsatisfying answers that students know are wrong but will share anyway.

7. Answer: The truck driver was walking, not driving. Riddles such as this illustrate how we work to come up with overly complicated narratives to explain evidence. With this riddle, expect your students to come up with elaborate stories to explain why a police officer would be so careless, such as the driver was rushing to the hospital, or was friends with the police officer. (One boy I worked with suggested that the two of them were accomplices in a bank robbery!)

8. Answer: The man was playing Monopoly. Like the previous riddle, this one will spur all kinds of imaginative stories to explain the situation. The simple solution will provide a real "ah-ha!" moment to your students.

After reviewing the answers to the riddles, ask students if they have changed their minds about which ones were easy and which were hard. Discuss how the riddles in the two columns were different. Elicit that the riddles in column 1 seemed easy, but actually should have made them stop and think, while the riddles in column 2 seemed to require a lot of thought to answer, when the solutions were actually simple. On the board, label the two columns of wrong answers: Column 1 "Thinking Fast," Column 2 "Thinking Slow."

Wrap Up

Point out to students that the wrong answers for column 1 were the result of "fast thinking" that was *too* fast, and that wrong answers in column 2 were the result of "slow thinking" that got them bogged down.

Have students brainstorm times in their own lives in which fast thinking or slow thinking got them in trouble. Elicit that fast thinking can cause you to jump to conclusions, and this can cause you to make simple mistakes in school work or on tests—and to get into conflicts with family and friends. Slow thinking, on the other hand, can make you dwell too much on problems—both in school work and in your personal life.

Extending the Lesson

Now that you have experientially introduced students to the concept of fast thinking (quick and intuitive responses) and slow thinking (responses that are the result of labor-intensive logical thought), you can use those terms as shorthand for types of cognitive distortions you will be discussing in other contexts throughout this book (such as *jumping to conclusions* and *automatic thoughts* as examples of fast thinking and *over-elaborate explanations of others' motives* as an example of slow thinking).

Relationships

"YOU CAN'T GIVE UP ON YOUR FAMILY, NO MATTER HOW TEMPTING THEY
MAKE IT . . ."

FROM *THE SEA OF MONSTERS*, BY RICK RIORDAN

Social relationships matter. The connections we make, both as family members and as part of a community, are what make us human. What's more, the quality and quantity of our relationships profoundly affects our lifelong mental and physical health, and these effects begin in childhood and "cascade throughout life, to foster cumulative advantage or disadvantage in health" (Umberson & Monetz, 2010). In short, interpersonal relations determine the quality of our lives, for good or bad. Helping students develop the skills to develop and maintain healthy, satisfying relationships is key to social and emotional learning.

Of course, our first and most profound set of relationships are with family members. Navigating the complex relationships we have with our family is a challenge that lasts a lifetime (or beyond—just ask the ancient Greek god Hermes from the Percy Jackson series, quoted above!). Family relationships are never more difficult than when we enter our teen years. In the first portion of our exploration of relationships, we are going to look at ways to help young teens manage their closest, most personal social relationships: those they have with their families.

It's no mystery why the family relationship can be so challenging for young teens. Remember, puberty is the stage at which children begin to forge a separate identity, and a large part of that process entails asserting their independence from their parents. Managing the transition to independent self-hood, while still maintaining a strong sense of belonging to the family, is a major challenge for students in their middle school years.

This tension between independence and family identity is reflected in young adult literature, which is filled with heroes and heroines struggling to forge an independent identity while maintaining the sense of belonging that a family provides. Novels like *The Giver* or *The Hunger Games* show us heroes struggling to fit into societies where family life is a trap, and any sense of individuality is crushed. At the other end of the spectrum, we find free agents like Huckleberry Finn or Harry Potter—orphans whose fantastic journeys are basically a search for the sense of belonging that a family provides. Family dynamics are also at the heart of any number of realistic young adult novels, running the gamut from Liesel's harrowing relationship with her foster parents in war-torn Germany in *The Book Thief* to the goofy conflicts between Greg Heffley and his brothers in the Diary of a Wimpy Kid series.

What Is a "Peer" Anyway?

Peer—it's a pretty broad term. Social psychologists often describe adolescent peer relationships as falling into three categories, depending on the closeness of the relationships (Turner, 1996):

Friendships are one-on-one relationships in which teens help each other, share personal thoughts and feelings, cooperate, and comfort one another.

Cliques are small groups of three to 12 individuals, and average five or six members. Cliques form among individuals from similar backgrounds who also hold similar interests, attitudes, and beliefs. Membership in a clique can be highly exclusive, and members usually come into contact every day.

Crowds are larger and less intimate groups of individuals who share common interests and socialize together. Membership in a crowd offers boys and girls the chance to interact socially in a relatively low-pressured environment. A crowd will often be identified with a broad descriptive label, such as jocks, stoners, skaters, geeks, and so on. Often, belonging to a clique will be an informal "ticket" for acceptance in a larger crowd.

See if you can identify from day to day the various crowds and cliques among the teens you deal with.

In this unit are activities for mapping family ties, exploring family dynamics, and recognizing the importance of appropriate boundaries. Use them as tools for analyzing literature, when appropriate. You can also use them as tools to get students thinking about—and writing about—their own family relationships.

After family, our most important relationships are with our friends and romantic partners. During the middle school years, those out-of-family relationships become more intense, dramatic, and central to the young teen's life. Cliques and crowds, first dates and silent crushes, BFFs and bullies—there is a ton of drama on the middle school social calendar!

There's a whole library of research to back up what everyone who works with young teens knows well: Children become more and more influenced by peers as they begin the transition into adolescence. Peer influence on a child's behavior and emotions "peaks in the first years of adolescence, then gradually declines as teens adjust their relationships with parents and develop a more mature sense of autonomy" (Fuligni, Barber, Eccles, and Clements, 2001). Specifically, research has found that as children move from the elementary school years to middle school, the importance of companionship and intimacy with peers increases as it decreases with parents, and this is reflected by greater self-disclosure with peers and less with parents. Basically, as teens grow closer with friends, their relationship with parents grow less close (Buhrmester & Furman, 1987).

So peer relationships—whether intimate friendships or membership in cliques and "crowds"—are a key element in a middle schooler's social and emotional functioning. This is certainly reflected in young adult literature. From contemporary fantasy series, like The Mortal Instruments or Twilight, to more realistic explorations of friendship and romance, peer connections and conflicts are at the heart of stories middle schoolers love to read.

The unit ends with a look at the moral development of middle schoolers. It provides some ideas for lessons to help them sort out their notions of right and wrong, and ends with a lesson that challenges students to consider the emotional states that underlie "rude" behavior. Understanding the emotional dimension of behavior is key to developing pro-social actions and attitudes.

Social & Emotional Learning © 2014 by Tom Conklin, Scholastic Teaching Resources

Parents—How They Help Students Achieve

"When I was a boy of fourteen, my father was so ignorant that I could hardly stand to have the old man around. But when I got to be twenty-one, I was astonished at how much he had learned."

—Mark Twain

Study after study confirms that parental involvement has a positive effect on student performance in middle school. Yet that fact seems contrary to the common adolescent attitude toward parents captured by the Mark Twain quote, above. How does parental involvement benefit students who are beginning to indulge in teenage rebellion against their parents? A recent analysis of 50 studies found that not all parental involvement is equal, and that certain interventions have much greater positive impact on student outcomes than do others (Hill & Tyson, 2009).

The analysis found that of all the different kinds of parental involvement studied, only direct involvement in homework was *not* linked to increased success by middle school students. Apparently, having parents checking to make sure that all homework is done—or, even worse, parents helping out with the homework—is no guarantee of student achievement! Parental involvement in school activities—such as volunteering at bake sales or attending school concerts or plays—was only weakly linked to academic achievement. By far, the most effective type of parental involvement entailed what the study's authors call "academic socialization"—that is, parental actions that help their kids figure out what school is all about. This includes the following:

• Clearly communicating expectations for achievement
• Discussing learning strategies (such as note-taking and summarizing)
• Talking about the purposes, goals, and meaning of education
• Linking school work with future plans and career goals

The result of "academic socialization" will be students who *choose* to do their best. So communicate to parents that if they truly want to use their parental authority to help their kids achieve, they should focus less on *when* and *how* the homework gets done, and focus more on *why* homework is important. The kids can take it from there.

Social Context

"IT TAKES A VILLAGE TO RAISE A CHILD."

So says the old proverb. And it's true: the social context in which we come of age plays a big part in determining what kind of people we turn out to be. Gaining awareness of the social context in which they are living is a key element of children's social and emotional development. How can we model this in a way that a young teen can grasp? It helps to think of a bull's-eye.

The social scientist Urie Bronfenbrenner constructed an ecological model of human development that uses concentric circles to represent the various social systems in which human development takes place. Bronfenbrenner identified five environmental systems in which each individual child develops, with each of those systems depicted as a ring in the circles surrounding the child.

In the "bull's-eye" of Bronfenbrenner's model is the child.

The next ring, closest to the child, is the *microsystem*, which refers to the child's immediate environment, including family, school, and friends.

The next ring Bronfenbrenner calls the *mesosystem*, which is a "system of systems." It represents the interactions between different elements of the microsystem (family, school, church) and the community at large.

The mesosystem links the inner circle to the *exosystem*. This represents the "village" in the "it takes a village" proverb. It covers neighbors, local government, and other local institutions not directly interacting with the child.

The ring farthest from the child is the *macrosystem*, which Bronfenbrenner refers to as "large-scale patterns of culture." This includes such things as national customs, the economy, national politics, and the mass media.

Finally, Bronfenbrenner identifies the *chronosystem* as an important element of development. This refers to how the individual and her environment changes over time (Bronfenbrenner, 1994, pp. 37–43).

Bronfenbrenner's model has the advantages of being both comprehensive and intuitive. It gives teens a way to grasp the different "layers" of the society they live in, with themselves and their families at the center. The following mapping activity adapts Bronfenbrenner's model into a self-directed learning experience for students.

LESSON 6

Circles of Myself

SEL Objectives: 8, 15

Preparing for the Lesson

Make copies of Worksheet 6: Circles of Myself (page 104). Gather colored markers or highlighter pens for students to use.

Warm Up

Ask students whom they are closest to. Whom do they know best? Who knows them the best? Have them consider the question in very practical terms: Whom do they see and talk to most often? Is there anyone they consider themselves close to, but whom they hardly ever talk to?

Using the Lesson

1. Distribute the worksheet. Have students fill it out with the names of people they have relationships with. Tell them to categorize people as follows:

   - In the center circle, students write words to describe themselves, such as their likes, dislikes, and future plans.

   - People they are closest to go in "My Inner Circle."

   - People they know, but are not close to, go in "My Outer Circle."

   - People they hardly know go in the last circle.

   - People they know about, but who do not know them (e.g., celebrities, the President), go on the worksheet outside of the circles.

2. If it's appropriate with your class, ask them if they have seen the movie *Meet the Parents*. (This is a favorite with most middle schoolers I've worked with.) Point out that the inner circle is like the "circle of trust" that Robert DeNiro's character kept referring to. Ask them who is in their circle of trust. How do people make it into that inner circle?

3. When they have placed the names in the circles have students discuss their Circles of Myself. Which of their circles is most crowded? Which one is least crowded? What does this say about them? (e.g., "I'm a private person" or "I have a lot of people close to me.")

4. Distribute the colored markers or highlighters and have students use them to indicate the type of relationship they have with each person. For instance, they could use green to indicate family members, blue to indicate friends, red to indicate non-family adults, such as teachers, coaches, priests/pastors, and so on. Discuss

whether students in which circles do most family members fall. Ask if there have been people they used to know but who are no longer on the chart. Why are those people gone?

5. Talk about which people on the chart they have known the longest. Which ones will they still know in five years? Ten years? Twenty? Are there people that they expect to add to their circles in the future? (e.g., a spouse and children of their own)

6. Elicit from students that family members are a constant in their Circles of Myself and will always be among the people they are closest to.

Wrap Up

Discuss with students the differences between friends and family. Share with them the common expression that says someone is "like family." What does it mean to be like family? Do you have to be related by blood to someone to be their family? Sum up the activity by having students write their own definition of family.

Extending the Lesson

Use the worksheet as a character map for works of literature. When studying a novel, students can use Circles of Myself to sort out the main character's various relationships.

Social & Emotional Learning © 2014 by Tom Conklin, Scholastic Teaching Resources

The Family Tree

Once students have mapped out all of their relationships, they can focus their attention on family. A genogram is a simple, engaging tool for mapping out family relationships and history. It was developed in the mid-1980s by renowned family therapists Monica McGoldrick and Randy Gerson and publicized in their book *Genograms: Assessment and Intervention.*

A variation on the traditional family tree, a genogram includes details on the relationships between family members over generations. When used by physicians or mental health professionals, a genogram is a powerful diagnostic tool for uncovering patterns of illness or psychological problems. For our purposes, we will use genograms as a tool for having students express their cultural and ethnic heritage, while also researching how various members of their families have interacted over the years.

MODERN FAMILY

The dictionary tells us that a family is a group consisting of parents and children living together in a household. The traditional family consists of a married husband and wife raising their own offspring. This arrangement, while still common, is far from being the only type of family in today's society. In fact, according to the 2010 census, only 20 percent of American households consisted of married couples with children (U.S. Census Bureau, 2012).

So, what does family mean in a culture in which nearly half our children are being raised by single parents, grandparents, adoptive parents, or step-parents? How can we define the term so that *all* children can identify with the positive qualities of family life, not just those children being raised in a traditional household?

World-renowned child psychiatrist Salvador Minuchin came up with a flexible definition of family that works well to describe any number of domestic arrangements. According to Minuchin, a healthy family is a *system*. Each family system provides its members with a sense of belonging, encourages each member to be autonomous individuals, and accomplishes both of these goals while remaining flexible enough to adapt to change (Stein, Mozdzierz, and Mozdzierz, 1998). "The family is the natural context for both growth and healing," according to Minuchin (Minuchin, 1981, p. 11). In other words, "family" may be defined as an intimate, flexible social group that offers each of us a sense of belonging, while also affording us the freedom to be ourselves.

LESSON 7

Genograms

SEL Objectives: 8, 15

Preparing for the Lesson

Provide students with large sheets of construction paper or butcher paper, along with colored markers, that they can use to construct their genograms. You may also wish to make available geometric shape templates that students can use to make neat circles and squares for their genograms. (Staedtler templates are a good choice, as they also provide a straight edge for drawing lines on the genograms.)

Make copies of Worksheet 7: Genograms (page 105).

Warm Up

Ask students if they know what a family tree is. Elicit that it is a chart that shows how different generations of family members are related to each other. Tell them that they are going to make their own family tree.

Using the Lesson

1. First, set the limits for the genograms. In order to keep them manageable, I suggest having students focus on three generations: themselves and their siblings, their parents, and their grandparents.

2. On a sheet of paper, have students make a list of the names of people in each of these three generations in their family. Have them include aunts and uncles in their parents' generation. It's best to have them restrict their list to their grandparents, as adding grand-aunts and grand-uncles is likely to make their genograms overly complicated. Make sure that students include family members who have passed away on their lists.

3. After students have finished their lists, distribute the construction paper and markers. Tell students they are going to use their lists to create a genogram.

4. Write the word *genogram* on the board and use slashes to separate it into syllables (gen/o/gram). Ask them what other words start with *gen-* (focus on words such as *generation, genetics, genealogy*). Point out that the word root *gen* has to do with family, tribe, or race. Next, ask for words that end with *-gram* (such as *diagram, telegram*). Point out that the suffix *-gram* indicates something written, drawn, or otherwise recorded. Ask students to explain what a genogram is. (a diagram that shows a family)

5. Next, distribute copies of Worksheet 7. (You may also want to draw the genogram symbols on the board.) Tell students to use the symbols and their lists of relatives to start a basic genogram of their family. Share with them the following instructions:

- Use squares to represent males and circles to represent females.

- The genogram will show three rows, with each row presenting a different generation.

- The top row shows grandparents.

- The middle row shows parents, aunts, and uncles.

- The bottom row shows the student, along with the student's siblings.

- When showing siblings the oldest child goes farthest left, the youngest farthest right, with any children in between shown from older to younger.

    Give students plenty of time to organize and construct their basic genogram. (Students from large families may have to simplify theirs by eliminating aunts and uncles.)

6. After students have finished their basic genograms, tell them that they will next add some detail to the genograms. Specifically, they will add ethnic background and relationship background.

Ethnic background: Have students select colors to represent the ethnic backgrounds of their family members and to trace each family member's symbol accordingly. For instance, they might choose to represent African Americans with the color blue, and Italian Americans with the color red. If an African American grandfather married an Italian grandmother, their children would be outlined in blue and red. Their grandchildren would be outlined in blue and red, plus additional colors for any other ethnicity from the other parent's side of the family. As they get to the current generation, the genograms are apt to get very colorful!

Relationship background: Tell students that they are to draw lines connecting family members. Point out that the shape of the line will show the main characteristic of the relationship. While genograms used by family therapists show a wide variety of relationships patterns (including fused, abusive, and so on), for our purposes we will include marital status and the following attitudes toward each other:

- Close/Loving

- Distant

- Hostile

- Cut off

Students might not be able to complete this when it comes to their parents' and grandparents' generations. Give students the homework assignment to interview either their parents or grandparents in order to learn more about the family relationships. Share with students these interviewing techniques:

- Ask open-ended questions, not yes/no questions.

- Ask about specific incidents, not just general attitudes.

- "Tell me a story about . . ." is a great way to get information about family.

Students should complete the genograms after their interviews. If they want to expand the genogram to include other family members, such as second cousins, grand-aunts, and grand-uncles, based on information they have learned, encourage them to do so at this time.

Wrap Up

Process what students have learned about their families. Did they learn anything that surprised them? Did they discover any traits? Have them count the number of ethnic backgrounds that are shown on their genogram. What ethnicity do they consider themselves to be?

If appropriate, suggest that students could also use the genogram to indicate illnesses, such as diabetes or heart disease, in the family. Point out that doctors use genograms to spot patterns in families in order to help prevent illness.

Extending the Lesson

Genograms can be used to map out relationships in fiction, especially serial novels. Students who are fans of the Harry Potter or Twilight novels will enjoy coming up with elaborate genograms to describe their favorite characters and their relationships.

Family Dynamics

Think of the word *dynamics*, and what comes to mind? Actions and motions, stressors and pressures. It's a term from physics and mechanical engineering. So why do we use *dynamics* to describe families?

As mentioned earlier, experts describe a family as a system, not a static collection of individuals. Tools like a genogram or Bronfenbrenner's concentric circles are handy ways to visualize how the different parts of a family are related, but how can we understand how the family works? If a family is a system, not a thing, then how can we understand what makes that system tick?

Virginia Satir, a noted family therapist, uses the metaphor of a mobile to represent the family. Like a mobile, a family consists of many different parts, each a different size and shape. Also like a mobile, a family system hangs in a delicate balance. If something happens to one of the pieces, it causes a ripple effect throughout the entire structure as the different pieces twist and shift until a new balance is achieved. In a family system, says Satir, the equivalent of the mobile's strings and struts are family rules and communication patterns (Satir, 1972, pp. 119–120).

Family Rules

Every family has its rules. These can vary from obvious household laws, such as bedtimes and limits on Internet use, to the unstated but understood routines that govern how parents and siblings interact. As youngsters age out of childhood and into adolescence, they naturally begin to test the rules that have determined their behavior in the home. This teen rebellion, while developmentally appropriate, can be the cause of lots of drama and angst. There's nothing to send the "family mobile" spinning like a teenager testing the family rules! Much family dysfunction is a direct result of family members—teens included—either flouting healthy family rules or rigidly enforcing rules that do not serve a positive purpose in the family's life.

You may feel the need to proceed with great caution when dealing with family matters in an academic setting, and with good cause. (Teaching is not counseling, after all!) Still, family relationships are central to a student's emotional and social development. The family setting offers a familiar and immediate context in which to explore with teenagers the concept that they are part of a social system, and their actions affect other people.

Let's explore a dimension of family dynamics that has implications throughout the spectrum of social and emotional learning: boundaries.

Boundaries

Ask a 13-year-old to define the term *boundary*, and you'll get a variety of answers. The border between Mexico and the United States, the fence surrounding a swimming pool, the lines on the page of a coloring book that the young artist is supposed to "stay inside of"—these are all examples of boundaries as a typical young teen understands them. But what counts as a boundary in our personal lives? Grasping that concept is more of a challenge.

Minuchin, writing about family systems, suggests that boundaries can be sorted into different types, depending on how they function.

RIGID boundaries are reflected in hard-and-fast rules and roles. In families, rigid boundaries are often set by parents seeking to maintain control over their child's behavior. Teen rebellion is often a reaction to rigid boundaries that were established during the teen's childhood years and kept up as they enter adolescence.

CLEAR boundaries are firm but appropriate, with all parties understanding the reasons that inform those boundaries. Clear boundaries are also flexible and can evolve as family members change over time.

DIFFUSE boundaries result in a situation in which family rules are inconsistent or non-existent, and family roles become blurred. Minuchin popularized the term "enmeshed" to describe those family system in which the roles of parents and children are diffuse, and where everyone in the family gets into each other's business with no sense of boundaries at all (Minuchin, 1974, pp. 53–56).

The following exercise provides students with an introduction to the concept of boundaries and the three basic types of boundaries described by Minuchin.

LESSON 8

Boundaries

SEL Objectives: 5, 7, 15, 17

Preparing for the Lesson
Make copies of Worksheet 8: Boundaries (page 106). (This critical-thinking exercise is appropriate for small-group work.)

Warm Up
Ask students what the word *boundary* means and have them give examples of boundaries. If they restrict their definitions to physical boundaries, such as national borders, direct the discussion on boundaries as they pertain to relationships. What

Social & Emotional Learning © 2014 by Tom Conklin, Scholastic Teaching Resources

boundaries do they have in their families? In school? With friends? Do boundaries always stay the same, or do they change over time? If they do change, how do they change? Then distribute Worksheet 8 to students.

Using the Lesson

1. First, have the class as a whole review the three types of boundaries described on the worksheet. Ask students to give personal example of each of the three types.

2. Next, have students work together in pairs or small groups to evaluate the 15 boundaries listed on the worksheet and decide which of the three types each boundary is. Some are obvious ("Beware of Dog!" is rigid) while others are open to interpretation ("Do unto others . . ."). When students working in teams disagree on which type any of the boundaries may be, have them talk through their disagreement until they reach a consensus. Give students 10 to 15 minutes to work their way through the list.

3. Have students share their answers. As before, if there is disagreement over classifying a boundary, allow discussion until there is consensus.

Wrap Up

Go over the questions at the end of the worksheet. Ask what life would be like if there were no boundaries. Are there boundaries that are frustrating but still important? What makes a boundary important?

Allow students who are willing to share to discuss boundaries in their own homes. Who sets those boundaries? How are they communicated? Are these boundaries clear? Rigid? Fuzzy?

Extending the Lesson

Work with students to create a comprehensive list of classroom boundaries. You might organize your list in these categories:

Physical: No physical contact, respect each other's personal space, etc.

Behavioral: No speaking out of turn, listen respectfully, no distracting behavior, etc.

Academic: No copying of each other's work, turn in work on time, etc.

Friendship

Harry Stack Sullivan, an important figure in the history of American psychiatry and founder of the interpersonal school of psychoanalysis, identified first friendships as a milestone in the development of the individual personality. According to Sullivan, a child's first friendship is qualitatively different from the child's relationship with parents. Sullivan claims that a child's first friendship marks the first time he ever places another person's emotional well-being above his own, without expecting something in return:

> "All of you who have children are sure that your children love you; when you say that, you are expressing a pleasant illusion. But if you will look very closely at one of your children when he finally finds a chum . . . you will discover something very different in the relationship—namely, that your child begins to develop a real sensitivity to what matters to another person . . . nothing remotely like this appears before the age of, say, eight-and-a-half, and sometimes it appears decidedly later" (Sullivan, 1953, pp. 244–246).

What, exactly, does friendship provide a young teen? Social scientists have studied friendship as a phenomenon and come up with lists of traits and behaviors of friendship (Wright, 2000, pp. 702–703).

One approach is to identify friendship *behaviors*:

COMPANIONSHIP: "Hanging out"
CONSIDERATION: "Being there" for each other
COMMUNICATION: Sharing thoughts, beliefs, dreams
AFFECTION: Sharing positive emotions for each other

Another approach is to think of friendship *values*:

UTILITY: Helping each other out
STIMULATION: Having fun together
SUPPORT: Providing encouragement and downplaying setbacks
AFFIRMATION: Reinforcing a friend's self-worth
SECURITY: Making a friend feel safe and trusted

Making young teens aware of these benefits and responsibilities of friendship can help them form and maintain friendships that are satisfying and endure. The traits of friendship also underlie healthy romantic relationships, and consciously cultivating those traits in friendships will provide teens with relationships that can serve as a template for romantic attachments based on more than infatuation.

In the following activity, teens use their critical-thinking skills to identify the traits of friendship and express them in their own words. They then use writing prompts, which present the above-listed friendship behaviors and benefits in "teen-friendly" terms and challenge teens to compose an autobiographical essay sharing examples from their own life experiences.

LESSON 9

What Do Friends Do?

SEL Objectives: 1, 8, 9, 17

Preparing for the Lesson

Make copies of Worksheet 9: What Do Friends Do? (page 107).

Warm Up

Write the word *friend* on the board. Have students brainstorm a list of words that they associate with the term and record them on the board, making a word map that has to do with the concept of *friend*. Challenge students to come up with as many synonyms for *friend* as possible (e.g., *bud, pal, bestie, homie, bff, bro, girl*). Ask students to differentiate between these different "flavors" of friends. (If your students are anything like the young teens I have worked with, they will have very strong opinions on the differences between a bud, a bro, and a bestie, for starters!) Also ask for antonyms for the word *friend* (e.g., *enemy, stranger*). What differentiates the two? (Strangers are neutral, while enemies are people with whom you have hostile relationships.) Mention the term *acquaintance* and have volunteers talk about the differences between friends and acquaintances. This can lead to a discussion of what friends do for each other. How do we know when someone is a friend? What do we get out of friendships? How many close friends do you have? Is it possible to have lots of close friends? Why or why not? (See the box "The Friend Zone" on page 49.)

Ask students if they have heard the expression "to have friends you must be a friend." Explain that they are going to think about and write about how to be a friend.

Using the Lesson

1. Distribute Worksheet 9. Have volunteers take turns reading each point on the worksheet. As they read the points, have volunteers describe examples of each from their own experiences.

2. The point that students might find most abstract and difficult to grasp is "Hold up a mirror to each other." Ask students to describe what a mirror does. (shows you a reflection of yourself) How do friends do that for each other? Does it mean that you only have friends who *look* like you? In what other ways are friends alike? (similar likes and dislikes, the same sense of humor, similar attitudes and communication styles)

3. As students discuss the points, have them reflect on how their friendships in middle school are like friendships they had when they were younger. How are they different? Do they have the same friends they had in first or second grade? If so, has the friendship changed or stayed the same over the years?

The essay assignment on the worksheet can be done as homework or an in-class assignment. Challenge students to make their essays as thematically integrated as possible. Point out that the challenge is to describe one or two incidents that demonstrate multiple points of friendship and not to simply write a laundry list to cover the points in order. Use the following rubric to evaluate student autobiographical friendship essays.

FRIENDSHIP ESSAY	3	2	1
Organization	The essay has a strong opening, a middle part that develops the theme, and an ending that sums up the essay and makes the reader think.	The essay has a good opening, middle, or end, but not all three. It either drags in one area or is undeveloped in others.	The essay is poorly structured. The parts do not flow together, and it is hard to follow.
Thoroughness	The essay covers all of the points on friendships discussed in preparation for the assignment.	The essay covers most of the points discussed, but omits some points and does not provide an explanation for why this is so.	The essay touches upon few if any of the points addressed in preparation for the assignment.
Thematic Integration	The essay is succinct and covers the points required in one or two personal anecdotes. It presents the material in an interesting and surprising way.	The essay covers its points in an uncreative, "laundry list" fashion. It gives a sense of the qualities of friendship but does not make those qualities really come alive.	The essay does not provide appropriate anecdotes to demonstrate the aspects of friendship it sets out to describe, or the examples provided to not match up with the qualities described.
Conventions	The essay has few if any misspellings or grammatical errors.	The essay has some misspellings and grammatical errors, but the author's meaning is clear.	The essay has misspellings and/or grammatical errors that make the author's meaning unclear.

GRADES: **A** 12–10 **B** 9–7 **C** 6–5 **D** 4

Wrap Up

Have students share their friendship essays with the classmate who is the subject of their work.

Extending the Lesson

Strong friendships are a staple of literature. Assign students to write a book report focusing on a novel that features a strong friendship. The book report should analyze the characters' friendship along the dimensions presented on the worksheet.

Social & Emotional Learning © 2014 by Tom Conklin, Scholastic Teaching Resources

Romance

To paraphrase P.T. Barnum, no one ever went broke by appealing to teenagers' obsession with romance. Pop music, movies, books, television series—they all exploit young love. The phenomenal success of the Twilight series is a case study of how teenagers' fascination with the opposite sex can be the cornerstone of a media empire. It's easy to see how a love triangle between a girl, a vampire, and a werewolf captured young imaginations around the world. Supernatural creatures, unable to control their urges? It's a perfect metaphor for the raging hormones and mysterious mood swings of adolescence. During a recent visit to a big-box bookstore, I saw that they now devote an entire section of the Young Adult area to "Paranormal Romance." While "paranormal" refers to those things that lie beyond the realm of science, the social sciences do provide some insight on the phenomenon of teen romance.

Social scientists study adolescent romance across different theoretical dimensions. One key distinction is between those who regard the topic according to a *behavioral* approach, and those who study teen romance according to *phase-based* models. Simply put, the behavioral systems approach considers *why* teens begin to explore romantic relationships by classifying the benefits teens gain by doing so. The phased-based model helps us understand the stages of teen relationships. One common phase-based model considers four distinct phases: *initiation, affiliation, intimate,* and *committed* (Meier & Allen, 2009).

Initiation: Marked by attraction, but with limited contact between the teens—AKA the "crush" phase.

Affiliation: The phase when teen boys and girls interact in group settings and start to learn how to interact with members of the opposite sex.

Intimate: This is when couples form and start to separate themselves from the group—the phase of first dates.

Committed: The phase when teens begin to explore physical and emotional intimacy.

The progression from crush, to group dates, to one-on-one dating, to "going steady," is appropriate and healthy. "Adolescent relationship experience is more than trivial puppy love," write the authors of the National Longitudinal Study of Adolescent Health (Meier & Allen, 2009). According to their findings, appropriate romantic experiences in the teen years are associated with healthier, more stable relationships in young adulthood and beyond.

Cliques and
Social Status/Peer Pressure

The words *mean girls* immediately bring an image to the mind's-eye: pampered, narcissistic teenage girls obsessed with fashion and status. Girls who proudly embrace their ruthless reputations, and who would do anything and hurt anyone in their quest to be at the top of their school's social food-chain.

Like so much in the teenage social milieu, the mean-girl stereotype is founded on a pop culture phenomenon—in this case, the hit Hollywood movie *Mean Girls*. Unlike a lot of other pop culture artifacts, the "mean girl" is not a purely fictional invention. "Adults find it funny. They are the ones who are laughing," says Tina Fey, who wrote the screenplay and appears in the film in the role of a supportive teacher. "Young girls watch it like it is a reality show. It's much too close to their real experiences, so they are not exactly guffawing" (Hobson, 2004).

Mean Girls comes across as a comic exaggeration of teenage social reality at least in part because it's based on a work of nonfiction: *Queen Bees and Wannabes* by Rosalind Wiseman. In her book, Wiseman explores the hierarchies commonly found in teen female cliques—a social milieu Wiseman calls "girl world." Like the characters in *Mean Girls*, inhabitants of "girl world" take on public roles that establish their function within their small clique of friends (Wiseman, 2002). Wiseman's insights on the social world of American high schools led to an entertaining movie, and her self-help books have been near the top of the best-seller lists. But is the depiction of an emotionally brutal, dog-eat-dog "girl world" accurate when it comes to middle school?

A study published by researchers at Yale University provides some perspective (Henrich, Kuperminc, Sack, Blatt, and Leadbeater, 2000). In the study, researchers conducted surveys and interviews with 499 middle school students in order to determine the relative percentage of students belonging to four social statuses: clique members; students with close one-to-one friendships; students with solid social ties but no clique membership or "best friend" relationship (what Wiseman calls "floaters"); and the socially isolated. The researchers then assessed how the students' social lives affected their behavior and school performance, along with the quality of their social relationships. Finally, the researchers compared results between boys and girls.

The results of the study are telling. In the study, 36 percent of boys and 25 percent of girls were "isolates," with no close friends; 15 percent of both boys and girls were in "best friend" relationships with a member of their own gender; 15 percent of boys and 21 percent of girls were members of cliques; and 34 percent of boys and 40 percent of girls belonged to general "crowds" of friends. Analyzing the effects of social relationships on middle schoolers, the study confirms the idea that girls are more sensitive than boys to interpersonal concerns, and that membership in a clique is a common way for girls to satisfy their desire for popularity. Girls with fewer friends

Social & Emotional Learning © 2014 by Tom Conklin, Scholastic Teaching Resources

or no clique membership were prone to lower feelings of social competence and "relatedness," and were at greater risk of behavioral and academic troubles. This all tends to support the "girl world" thesis, in which popular girls shine at the expense of their less popular peers.

On the other hand, girls who belonged to cliques generally performed better socially and academically, which tends to undermine the theory that "girl world" cliques are hostile groups in which the Queen Bees run roughshod over their Wannabe peers. "Tightly knit groupings of interpersonally competent, trusting, and communicative friends may mutually validate the self-worth of group members," the study's authors write. "Although cliques are frequently stereotyped negatively . . . our overall findings suggest that clique membership is associated with consistently positive adaptive outcomes for girls (Henrich, Kuperminc, Sack, Blatt, and Leadbeater, 2000).

As for "boy world," the Yale study produced less clear results. Like the girls in the study, boys also joined cliques, but the boys' groups tended to be larger and more loosely knit than the girls' groups. In addition, there were no clear-cut benefits to clique memberships for boys, as measured by the researchers' assessments of social and emotional functioning. This could demonstrate that middle school boys place greater

The Friend Zone

Is there a limit to the number of people any one of us can honestly call "friend"? According to Oxford University anthropologist Robin Dunbar, the answer is yes, and the number of people any individual can call friend has been remarkably stable over the centuries.

According to Dunbar's research, we spend roughly 40 percent of our social time each week with up to five of the most important people we know. Those five people—our "inner circle"—represents just 3 percent of the 150 individuals that any human being can claim to have in his or her social world. (The figure of 150 people in any given person's social world has been dubbed "Dunbar's Number" in social science circles, and the number is fixed by our cognitive capacity.) "Since the time invested in a relationship determines its quality," Dunbar writes, "having more than five best friends is impossible when we interact face to face, one person at a time" (Dunbar, 2010).

Of course, these days, people have access to social media, which enables us to interact online any time, anywhere, not just in face-to-face interactions. Does incessant texting, tweeting, and so on alter the equation leading to Dunbar's Number? Not really—the average number of friends on a typical online profile is between 120 and 130—about the same number of people that would have been found in one's social circle in a small, rural community centuries ago (Dunbar, 2010).

value on independence and competition than do their female counterparts, or that the sort of satisfaction boys derive from hanging out in groups is not easily measured by the assessment tools used in the study (Henrich, Kuperminc, Sack, Blatt, and Leadbeater, 2000).

Of course, being in a teen clique isn't inevitably a positive experience. It's significant that the Yale study looked at middle school students, not high school teens. It could be that the negative effects of "girl world" portrayed by Wiseman and the movie *Mean Girls* are the result of older teens clinging to the sort of social behavior that served them better in the middle school years. Still, keep in mind that just because cliques can be brutal for girls in the tenth grade doesn't mean that they're equally bad for girls in grade seven.

Another way to think about a middle schooler's social life is to apply the *sociometric status system*, which sorts children according to their popularity and social impact (Coie, Dodge, and Coppotelli, 1982). Here are the five most commonly identified statuses in the sociometric system:

POPULAR: A child often named as a best friend and rarely disliked

AVERAGE: Has an average number of friends and enemies

NEGLECTED: Not often picked as a friend but not actively disliked

REJECTED: Rarely picked as a friend and often actively disliked

CONTROVERSIAL: Often picked as a best friend and also often disliked

Unlike the teen-centric roles in "girl world," these statuses cross genders and can be identified in children starting in preschool (Coie, Dodge, and Coppotelli, 1982). They also correlate to behavior, with rejected and controversial children more likely to act aggressively and be at higher risk of juvenile delinquency. There is also a link between sociometric status and school performance. One study found, to its authors' surprise, that middle-schoolers in the "neglected" category had better academic profiles than other types of students. The authors suggest that this is because neglected kids were more motivated to succeed in school and were usually better liked by their teachers than by other kids (Wentzel & Asher, 1995).

Teachers may wish to pay attention and try to determine which of the social statuses each student occupies, and how it is affecting that student's academics. Keep in mind that "controversial" students—generally not a teacher's favorite (Wentzel & Asher, 1995)—have leadership strengths that can be cultivated in classroom activities. "Average" children could be more likely to fall through the cracks of unrealized potential than those "neglected" bookworms. And "rejected" children sometimes need just a little added attention to break through.

After this brief look at teen social groups and statuses, it's easy to see how peer pressure to conform is a powerful force in any middle schooler's life; in fact, research indicates that the social pressure to conform peaks at around the eighth or ninth grades

Social & Emotional Learning © 2014 by Tom Conklin, Scholastic Teaching Resources

(Leventhal, 1994). It's important to recognize that peer pressure is not necessarily a negative influence on a middle schooler. Yes, it can cause an impressionable "average" boy to follow in the bad behaviors of a more "controversial" peer, but it can also encourage open and supportive communication among a group of friends who do not want to let each other down.

What's more, recent brain research suggests that physiology is to blame, at least in part, for why young teens are so susceptible to peer pressure. Neuroscientists have discovered that the reward system in the mid-brain region develops more rapidly than the decision-making area of the prefrontal cortex, and the rush of neurotransmitters when a teen feels acceptance from peers can more than offset his ability to accurately assess the consequences of his actions in doing so. Remove the emotional stimulation of a peer-pressure situation, and teens can make decisions that are as rational as an adult's (Wang, 2003).

Socially, physically, emotionally, the cards are stacked in favor of teens giving in to peer pressure. Recognizing this, it's clear that simply hectoring teens to "just say no" to peer pressure can be useless, or even counter productive if defying adult pressure increases their acceptance among peers. What's more, that approach frames "peer pressure" as a grinding force at work on a passive victim—it doesn't address the fact that peer pressure cuts both ways, and young teens exert it as well as endure it.

Instead of dwelling on the negative and passive aspects of peer pressure, I prefer to make young teens mindful of the fact that they feel and exert peer pressure, and encourage them to strive to use their powers for good. The following exercise plants the seed that peer pressure is a potent force, and that yielding to it and exercising it are both choices.

LESSON 10

Feel the Force

SEL Objectives: 1, 5, 7, 9, 12, 16, 17

Preparing for the Lesson
Make copies of Worksheet 10: Feel the Force (page 108).

Warm Up
Tell students that there was a popular book called *How to Win Friends and Influence People*. Ask them to think about how people influence other people. Challenge students to come up with specific examples of how they have either influenced or been

> **TIP** Many middle school students have already been exposed to the concept of peer pressure, and almost always in a negative context. As a result, those rebellious teens most prone to giving in to negative peer pressure might resist considering the topic when it is explicitly presented to them. For that reason, I suggest couching this topic in terms of "the Force" by which people influence each other, only bringing up "peer pressure," as such, at the very end.

influenced by other people. (Possible responses may range from "they talk you into stuff" to "they threaten you" to "they make you feel bad if you don't do something.") Explain that they are going to think about ways that they use their own powers to influence other people.

Using the Lesson

1. Distribute Worksheet 10. It presents three areas of interpersonal relationships in which people exert influence over others:

   Friendship: the giving or withholding of affection. This is the emotional piece.

   Opinion: sharing positive or negative evaluations of the other person. This is where middle school students often engage in verbal aggression.

   Brain: the use of reason to persuade another person to act. Remember Kahneman's "System 2"—the slower, rational part of our thinking processes? This is where it is often put into play, to rationalize actions we want to make for purely emotional reasons.

   A key concept underlying this lesson is that any of these aspects of relationships lays along a continuum ranging from what I call "the good side" to "the dark side." Any interpersonal exchange can be positive or negative, and it's up to us to choose how we interact with each other.

2. Have a volunteer read the introduction to the worksheet. Have other volunteers read the "Powers of the Force," starting with the middle column, then reading the examples from "The Good Side" and "The Dark Side."

3. Take time to discuss each of the "Powers" before moving on to the next one. Have students volunteer examples from their own experience of "good" and "bad" examples of each "Force."

4. After going over each of the three "Powers of the Force," ask which of the three powers the students think is strongest: friendship, other people's opinions, or powers of persuasion. Then ask whether "The Good Side" or "The Dark Side" is strongest. Do people respond more to threats and disrespect or to affection and encouragement?

5. Have students work in small groups to complete the lesson by coming up with examples of "the Force" in action. Each group should pick one of the situations presented and write a short scene or skit dramatizing how the characters in the scene influence each other.

6. Challenge students to include each of the three "Powers of the Force" in their scene, with a mix of positive and negative examples. Suggest the following checklist for them to follow as they plan and write their skits:

- Where is the scene set?

- Who are the characters?

- What does each character want from the other characters?

- How do the characters try to influence each other? Be sure to use all three "Powers of the Force."

- How does the scene end? Who influenced whom?

7. Students can perform their skits for each other. After each skit, have class members identify how each of the three "Powers of the Force" were dramatized.

Wrap Up

After the in-depth exploration of this topic, introduce the concept of peer pressure. Ask how the different powers students use to influence other people work in terms of peer pressure. Ask students how they can be accepted by their peers without crossing over to the "The Dark Side."

Extending the Lesson

Have students use their worksheets to identify how the "Powers of the Force" are used by characters on TV shows. (Popular sitcoms that feature teen characters offer excellent case studies for how peer pressure influences characters.) Have students watch a show and keep track of how the different "Powers" are used. Students who watched the same show can then compare notes to see if they identified the same "Powers" at work.

Moral Development

Anyone who has spent much time with young teens knows just how passionate and certain they can be when it comes to sharing their views on what's good, what's evil, what's fair, and what deserves a beat-down. You can check in with the same teen a week later, and he can just as passionately defend the opposite point of view.

The middle school years are a period of great change in a child's life, and this is especially true in her moral development. What do we mean, exactly, by that? The textbook definition of moral development is "changes in thoughts, feelings, and behaviors regarding standards of right and wrong" (Santrock, 2012, p. 408). Not only are young teens going through upheavals in their physiology and their personal relationships, they are also in the process of reevaluating their basic notions of right and wrong. Let's take a look at why that is, and see how this tumultuous time of passage is really a chance for growth.

Social scientists and psychologists conceptualize morality along two fundamental dimensions: the *justice reasoning* approach, and the *care reasoning* approach (Peterson & Seligman, 2004). The justice approach views our notions of right and wrong as essentially products of our rational minds, and as our cognitive skills develop over time, so do our moral judgments. The care perspective considers morality through the lens of emotion. Basically, the justice approach sees the question of right and wrong as an act of judgment made according to abstract principles. The care approach sees morality as rooted in compassion and informed by a person's sense of what will best serve the needs of others.

Current research indicates that we make our moral decisions by applying a combination of justice and care concerns, and that moral development takes place in stages, like Piaget's cognitive stages of development (Peterson & Seligman, 2004). Now let's take a closer look at those stages, and see where middle-schoolers fit in.

THE STAGES AND LEVELS

Harvard psychologist Lawrence Kohlberg identified three levels of moral development: preconventional, conventional, and postconventional. Each of those levels is comprised of two stages, with a total of six potential stages of moral development. The chart (opposite) lays out the levels and stages, giving their characteristics.

The preconventional stages are the moral province of the preschool and elementary schools years. It's when learning that "sharing is caring" marks a significant leap in moral understanding, and "fairness" in rewards (and punishment) is the standard that kids hold most dear. It's at the ages of nine and ten when children begin to leave behind preconventional morality and embrace a moral worldview informed by personal loyalty and a proactive desire to do the right thing, and not merely to avoid punishment or get something in return. (It's significant that this is the same age when children form their first true friendships, according to Harry Stack Sullivan.)

Kohlberg referred to stage 3, interpersonal conformity, as the "good boy/good girl stage," but I think that's a little misleading. Many middle schoolers do not make their moral decisions in order to be seen as a "good boy" or "good girl" by the adult world; they choose to act in order to please and protect the people they care about the most.

What does all of this mean for your students? If they are typical middle schoolers, most of them will be at level 2, stage 3 of Kohlberg's model.

Level 1 • Preconventional	Level 2 • Conventional	Level 3 • Postconventional
Stage 1 Punishment and Obedience Children obey because adults tell them to. *"Might makes right."*	Stage 3 Interpersonal Conformity Trust, caring, loyalty are the basis for moral decisions. *"I mean well, and that's what counts."*	Stage 5 Social Contract Individuals have rights that must be protected. *"What brings the most good to the most people?"*
Stage 2 Instrumental Exchange People pursue their own interests and let others do the same. *"You scratch my back, I'll scratch yours."*	Stage 4 Social Conformity Moral decisions are based on understanding of social order, law, and duty. *"Law and order."*	Stage 6 Universal Principles Moral judgments based on universal human rights. Individual conscience trumps law. *"Justice for all."*

(Kohlberg & Hersh, 1977)

Kohlberg assessed moral development by presenting his subjects with short stories that pose moral and ethical dilemmas. I've used his ethical dilemma scenarios as discussion-starters with groups of middle schoolers, which gives the kids a chance to think through their moral positions, clearly state them, and respectfully listen to other people's thoughts.

If you're interested in having discussions like this in your classroom, search the Internet using the terms *Kohlberg* and *dilemmas* to find many sources for these provocative stories. Also, having students come up with their own ethical dilemmas is a fun and thought-provoking writing exercise.

Rebel, Rebel

Holes, The Giver, The Chocolate War, City of Ember, The Hunger Games—these and other popular young adult books feature heroes who battle against unjust authority. Why do young teens respond so well to stories in which a teen wants to do the right thing, but comes to realize that means defying those in charge?

As they develop beyond the pre-conventional "might makes right" level of moral reasoning, children come to realize that "because I said so" is not a valid reason for obeying an authority figure. A young teen's increased capacity for abstract thought also results in his engaging in idealistic, "black and white" thinking. A fable like *The Giver* perfectly dramatizes how a young teen loses his innocent belief in the adult world's moral infallibility, while simultaneously discovering his personal sense of right and wrong.

Manners

"EVERY ACTION DONE IN COMPANY, OUGHT TO BE WITH SOME SIGN OF RESPECT TO THOSE THAT ARE PRESENT."

FROM *RULES OF CIVILITY*, A GUIDEBOOK
HAND-COPIED BY YOUNG GEORGE WASHINGTON

Obviously, the topic of manners is appropriate for a book on social and emotional learning. A healthy and positive set of habits that govern interactions with other people is key to social success. It's also an area where many young teens need guidance, to say the least. First, let's look at the difference between manners and etiquette.

The distinction between manners and etiquette is subtle, and most people think that the two words are interchangeable. Although the distinction may be subtle, it's important. Manners refers to the way people behave toward each other in social situations, with "good manners" referring to behavior that is considerate of other people's feelings. The quote at the top of this page, which was rule number one in the guidebook that young George Washington hand-copied as part of his education, sums up the essence of good manners: acting in a way that shows respects to others.

Etiquette, on the other hand, refers to rules and mores that society imposes on our behavior. It's a culture-bound phenomenon, and behavior that might be considered good etiquette in one culture could be considered offensive in others. Some social critics dismiss etiquette as a set of silly and arbitrary rules, and suggest that is a form of control, intended to impose social conformity (Battistella, 2009). There's something to that. Search the Internet for videos on etiquette, and you will find a trove of instructional movies from the 1940s and 1950s that present rules of behavior that today seem quaint, at best, and downright oppressive at worst. One from 1946, titled *How Do You Do?*, features a teenage girl upset over her many faux pas in introducing people to each other, until she comes to realize that it's a girl's duty to let males make introductions and start conversations!

Just as it's possible to obey the law and still treat people badly, it's also possible to closely follow all of the rules of etiquette yet still have callous and cruel manners. (Think of the dowager Lady Bracknell in *The Importance of Being Earnest*, proper in every respect and yet still able to cut a social "inferior" down to size with a single word.) On the other hand, someone can be kind and sympathetic, yet be clueless as to which fork to use or type of jacket to wear at a formal dinner. (Think of Huckleberry Finn bridling against Miss Watson's attempts to "sivilize" him with rules of behavior in polite society—a society built upon slave labor.)

Middle schoolers, as much as anyone, will see manners and etiquette as interchangeable. This presents a challenge. When I've brought up the topic of good manners, I've had young teens roll their eyes and groan that they just don't care about social "rules." Taking this attitude is a matter of pride for a lot of middle-school-aged kids, who are at the stage where they are trying to differentiate themselves from the adult world—flouting rules of etiquette gives them a relatively easy way to gain a sense of independence. However, teens have hypersensitive emotions, and at no point in our lives does the gold standard of manners—respect—mean more. Linking good manners to the social conformity of etiquette can lead teens to reject both and continue to behave in ways that hurt themselves and others. That's why it's important to clearly separate manners and etiquette when dealing with these subjects in middle school classrooms.

Here is a lesson on manners that inverts the usual formula for teaching rules of behavior. Instead of presenting rules of conduct that ought to be followed, the lesson looks at common examples of bad manners shown in a variety of contexts. It then challenges students to identify the negative emotions that cause people to behave in these rude and obnoxious ways. This approach helps teens to gain perspective on how their own behavior affects other people. It also gives them a chance to develop their ability to identify emotions and their consequences.

LESSON 11

How Rude!

SEL Objectives: 5, 7, 15, 17

Preparing for the Lesson
Make copies of Worksheet 11: How Rude! (page 109). This activity is appropriate for small-group work.

Warm Up
Ask students to describe the last time someone really got them angry. Odds are, they will describe incidents of rude behavior in which they were the target or victim. Challenge students to define *rude* in their own words. Then, group them together in teams of three to five to work on the activity.

Using the Lesson
1. Before starting, have a discussion on why people behave rudely. You are likely to hear students blame bad behavior on inherent qualities of the people who were rude. ("It's 'cause he's a jerk!" "She's just annoying.") Make sure that students understand the difference between who the person is and what the person does. Point out that people often act the way they do because of how they feel. Ask which emotions can cause people to be rude. Then, distribute the worksheet to the groups.

THE GOOD OLD DAYS?

"CHILDREN SHOULD BE SEEN AND NOT HEARD."

Many people long for the days when this was the rule guiding how young people behaved. Oh, for the days when children kept quiet in the presence of their elders, and only spoke when spoken to.

Well, things may have been that way once, somewhere. But the historical record indicates that American youngsters have been talkative, inquisitive, and not afraid to speak up, right from the earliest days of our nation.

Here's one example: In 1834, the British author Harriet Martineau made a visit to the United States and wrote a series of books about her travels called *Society in America*. She had a lot of unkind words to say about the American way of life, along with some keen insights. Martineau was very frank in her discussion of how American children behaved. "At Baltimore, a dozen boys and girls at a time crowded round me, questioning, discussing, speculating," she wrote. "In private houses, the comments slipped in at table by the children were often the most memorable." What did the prim British author make of the impertinent American children?

"I delighted in the American children," Martineau wrote. "The independence and fearlessness of [American] children were a perpetual charm in my eyes" (Martineau, 1837, pp. 166–167).

Yes, 1834 may qualify as the good old days, but clearly, having children be "seen and not heard" was not part of the equation. The moral of the story? Behavior that can be headstrong and even obnoxious in one context can also be fearless and independent, when properly channeled.

2. Tell students that these are common situations they experience, with examples of rude behaviors in each. Let a representative from each group read the behaviors from each situation, then have the class brainstorm other examples of rude behavior for each setting.

3. Next, have volunteers read each emotion and sample quote at the top of the page. Tell students that these are some emotions that can cause rude behavior, but add that there are other emotions that can result in rudeness. Encourage groups to add other emotions to the list if they think of any as they do the activity.

4. Do the first exercise as a class: "Making fun of the bus driver." Ask students which emotion can cause someone to do this, and why. Encourage more than one answer, and more than one interpretation for each answer. (e.g., "It could be anger, because the bus driver was rude first," "It's attitude, because they had a bad day at school," or "I think it's because they want to be the center of attention, and that's like

vanity.") After having a brief discussion of that example, tell students to work in their groups to fill in the blanks for the rest of the situations, and to supply reasons backing up each of their answers.

5. Circulate around the classroom as students work. Encourage them to come up with as many possible answers as they can think of, but to pick one that seems most common for each situation.

6. Near the end of the class, have each group "own" one of the situations. Let them report their answers and reasons to the class. As they do so, let other groups share if they had different answers or explanations for each situation. When there is disagreement, have the whole class vote on which answer they find most plausible.

Wrap Up

Finish the lesson by asking students how the activity they've been doing is really about good manners. Students will probably suggest it's because they have been talking about bad manners. Ask, "Based on this, what's a key to having good manners?" (controlling your negative emotions)

Ask students what is the common element of all the bad behaviors here. Elicit that each behavior shows a lack of respect for other people. Then ask, "What is the second key to having good manners?" (showing respect for other people)

Extending the Lesson

Use these situations as the basis for improv skits. Have students act them out, with the rude character picking which emotion is motivating his or her behavior. After each scene, have the other student guess which emotion the rude character was trying to represent.

Media

When a young teen isn't asleep or in school, what is she doing? Odds are, she'll be staring at a screen.

The numbers are startling. Out of every 24 hours, the typical American between the ages of 8 and 18 will spend approximately 11 hours using entertainment media. (Compare that to the 25 minutes per day that the average kid spends reading a book.) The "screen time" portion of all that media breaks down to:

- 4.5 hours watching TV

- 1.5 hours on a computer

- More than 1 hour playing video games on a console or handheld device (Rideout, Foehr, and Roberts, 2010)

In short, young teens are exposed to a lot of programming!

In this context, the word "programming" has two connotations. First, it literally refers to the shows and advertising that kids are exposed to; and second, all of this media consumption "programs" young viewers on how to act and react in social situations. To cite an obvious example, the link between exposure to media violence and violent behavior is one of the most studied topics in psychology. A recent study performed by an international team of researchers concluded that exposure to violent media over time does increase the likelihood of aggressive behavior (although that conclusion is fiercely disputed by others researchers). The researchers also found that exposure to media violence almost certainly desensitizes viewers to the consequences of violence (Krahe, Moller, Huesmann, Kirwil, Felber, and Berger, 2011).

The fact is that today's youth live in a media-saturated environment, and this affects their social and emotional functioning. Managing and limiting the amount of media that a young teen consumes is ultimately the parents' job, and yet it is possible for educators to help young teens develop the tools to emotionally process the hours of shows, music videos, movie clips, and advertising that they take in. All of that screen time presents an opportunity to cultivate their sensitivity to emotions, not just numb them to the suffering of others.

Advertising can be harnessed to focus teens' emotional awareness for a number of reasons. First, while many adults grumble about ads on TV, young teens actually tend to like commercials, and are more likely to watch them (Nielsen Company, 2009). (In my experience, middle schoolers with access to Internet videos will first try to watch music videos—when those are declared out of bounds, they're next most likely to watch favorite TV commercials.) Second, ads are almost always focused on evoking a specific emotional response in viewers, which makes it easier for young teens to recognize and identify the emotion targeted by the ad. And, finally, the emotions in an ad are always used in order to sell something. This provides an opportunity for young teens to examine how the things they watch on TV and in other media are *products*, created by people in order to manipulate the viewer's emotions and behavior. This critical-viewing skill is especially important today, with the overwhelming popularity of so-called reality shows—shows that present a distorted and artificial version of "reality."

Social & Emotional Learning by Tom Conklin © 2014 Scholastic Teaching Resources

UNIT 3

Emotional Management

> "...IF YOU CAN LEARN A SIMPLE TRICK, SCOUT, YOU'LL GET ALONG A LOT BETTER WITH ALL KINDS OF FOLKS. YOU NEVER REALLY UNDERSTAND A PERSON UNTIL YOU CONSIDER THINGS FROM HIS POINT OF VIEW—UNTIL YOU CLIMB INTO HIS SKIN AND WALK AROUND IN IT."
>
> FROM *TO KILL A MOCKINGBIRD*, BY HARPER LEE

It's no wonder that we often look back at middle school years as our "awkward phase." The transition from childhood to adulthood is not easy, and this can be reflected in a young teen's physical appearance—braces, gangly limbs, blemishes— all of the outward signs of a maturing body that can make a middle-schooler so painfully self-conscious. For many middle schoolers, the awkwardness of adolescence can run more than skin deep. The biological stresses of puberty, combined with the psychological challenges of searching for an identity while sorting out complicated relationships, may also present emotional and behavioral challenges.

Most often, young teens will naturally outgrow these inner problems, just as they outgrow their bad skin and obsessions with boy bands or collectible cards. But, in some cases, life stressors from the middle school years (or earlier) can lead the young teen to develop unhealthy habits, bad coping skills, or emotional problems that will negatively affect them for years to come. This unit will look at some of the challenges to effective social and emotional performance facing middle schoolers, along with activities to help them develop the awareness and skills to meet and overcome those challenges.

EMPATHY—THE NECESSARY CONDITION

The quote from *To Kill a Mockingbird* that opens this unit neatly defines the cornerstone of social and emotional learning: empathy.

My favorite clinical definition of *empathy* comes from the great psychotherapist Carl Rogers, who wrote that empathy means "to sense [another person's] private world as if it were your own, but without ever losing the 'as if' quality" (Rogers, 1957). This simple definition separates empathy from sympathy, in which we recognize *why* someone is feeling a powerful emotion without truly sharing that emotion. It also clearly differentiates empathy from a hyper-emotional state of emotional

enmeshment, in which someone wallows in a shared emotion without understanding or experiencing the reasons for the emotion.

If young teens are prone to that sort of wallowing in shared emotions, sometimes the adults in their lives find it challenging to move beyond sympathy and feel empathy for those teens. It may be difficult to feel empathy for an angry 13-year-old who acts out with disruptive behavior—but "climbing into his skin and walking around in it" might be a necessary step in helping that teen outgrow and overcome the hidden challenges that spark his unhealthy behavior.

Aggression

In her masterpiece *The Outsiders*, S.E. Hinton draws a vivid portrait of gang violence among the teens in a small Oklahoma city in the mid-sixties. Her portrayal of the conflict between the blue-collar Greasers and the well-off Socs is just as timely and real for young readers today as it was for the teens who read the novel when it was first published. Underneath the superficial veneers separating the Greasers from the Socs— and both of those gangs from teens in our own time—we can sense the pain, fear, and anger of real kids. Kids doing their best to survive in a hostile world.

Unfortunately, the world teens inhabit can still be a hostile place. Every year, the U.S. Department of Education and U.S. Department of Justice, in collaboration with the National Center for Education Statistics (NCES), publishes indicators of school crime and safety. The most recent report (Robers, Kemp, and Truman, 2013) presents some eye-opening statistics. According to the report:

- During the 2009–2010 school year, there were 1,396 homicides among youths ages 5–18. Nineteen of those homicides occurred at school.

- In 2011, students ages 12–18 suffered about 1,246,000 victimizations at school.

- In 2009–2010, about 74 percent of public schools reported one or more violent incidents of crime.

- Thirty-three percent of high schoolers reported being in at least one fight in 2011.

- That same year, 7 percent of high schoolers reported being threatened with a weapon on school property.

It's a sobering set of statistics, especially when you consider that it only reflects reported incidents of violence and crime. For every hostile act that makes it into a report like this, how many unreported acts of teasing, intimidation, and bullying do teens inflict on each other?

Let's take a brief look at what social scientists and neurologists have to say on the subject of teen aggression, then go over activities to help young teens better understand and manage their anger and aggression.

First, let's define our terms. Psychologists define *anger* as a person's response to a threat to himself or to a group with whom he identifies. Those threats can be either physical or psychological (e.g., "dissing" someone). Another necessary condition for anger is that the person feeling the emotion blames the other party for the threat (Lazarus, 1991). *Aggression* is defined as a behavioral act that results in harming or hurting others. That covers a lot of ground, so psychologists categorize aggression according to its context and the intent of the aggressor.

Here are common ways of categorizing aggression (Werner & Crick, 2004):

Social & Emotional Learning © 2014 by Tom Conklin, Scholastic Teaching Resources

PROACTIVE OR REACTIVE: Proactive aggression is goal-oriented and covers behaviors that run the gamut from stealing to teasing. Bullying is habitual proactive aggression. (See page 80.) Reactive aggression is done in response to real or perceived threats, and regulating it is a matter of impulse control. Reactive aggression is linked to peer rejection and victimization, while proactively aggressive kids are often seen as popular leaders.

OVERT OR COVERT: Overt aggression is clear to the aggressor, victim, and witnesses, while covert aggression is "sneaky," with victims at times being unaware of who is targeting them or why. Reactive aggression, by definition, is overt. Proactive aggression can be covert when it meets the needs of the aggressor.

PHYSICAL, VERBAL, OR RELATIONAL: Physical aggression—shoving, fighting, etc.—entails violence, and comprises most of the incidents that appear in the NCES statistics. Verbal aggression describes the teasing and taunts that often escalate into physical fights. With today's communication technologies, verbal aggression doesn't have to be overt or made in person—anonymous flames on social network sites are an extremely common form of bullying. Relational aggression refers to acts intended to destroy other people's social status and peer relationships (Werner & Crick, 2004). One teen boy I worked with described relational aggressive people as "psychological ninjas." "A classic bully wants to hurt you," he explained, "but a psychological ninja wants you to hurt yourself." Gossiping, rumor-spreading, and deliberate exclusion are prime examples of relational aggression (Kunimatsu & Marsee, 2012).

It's noteworthy that the most commonly studied forms of aggression are overt and physical; traditionally, the standard image of teen aggression has been the boy delinquent constantly getting into fights. While the "angry young male" stereotype still fits many teen aggressors, more girls today are acting out in physically aggressive ways. Also, social scientists are increasingly turning their attention to relational aggression, which is practiced more frequently by girls than boys (Lochman, Powell, Clanton, and McElroy, 2006).

So it's clear: Aggression is a problem for young teens, and it comes in many different forms from many different kinds of aggressors. But why is managing aggression such a major challenge for teens? Let's briefly focus on the physiological and psychological causes for adolescents' poor anger and aggression management skills.

In our explorations of emotions and peer pressure, we saw that the emotional centers of the brain—located in the subcortical region—develop more rapidly than the prefrontal cortex, which is home to the "executive" part of the brain. This discrepancy in neurological development plays a major role in the difficulty many teens have when it comes to controlling anger and aggression. One of the key regions of the brain is a small, almond-shaped region called the amygdala, buried in the center of the brain. There, it acts as a central switching area in the brain's limbic system, which is the seat of our emotions. A main function of the amygdala is what neuroscientists call the fear response system, which has evolved over the eons for a single purpose: survival. Whenever we sense danger, our amygdala fires up the fear response system, prompting one of three elemental responses: fight, flight, or freeze.

The limbic system evolved in order to help our ancient ancestors survive physical threats like snakes in the grass, but it also operates as we navigate social settings. After all, a threat is a threat—whether it comes from a literal snake in the grass, or a metaphorical "snake" planting nasty comments about you on the Internet! Psychologists link the three universal animal responses to danger with three coping styles used to respond to social stress: overcompensation (fight), avoidance (flight), and surrender (freeze) (Young, Klosko, and Weishar, 2003, pp. 26–37). Whenever we are in a social situation that triggers the fear response system, our limbic system will automatically signal us to immediately react by counter attacking, fleeing, or giving in. Thus, reactive aggression has been "hard-wired" in our brains over millions of years of evolution. Mature, well-adjusted minds are able to control initial crude emotional responses. But for young teens, whose brains are still developing, the reactive response is apt to be overwhelming—especially for those teens who have experienced trauma, abuse, or neglect.

If reactive aggression is linked to the brain's fear response system, then what physiological system is involved in proactive aggression? Remember, the hallmark of proactive aggression is that it is goal-oriented; it is a conscious choice, made to achieve an end. The neocortex (the "executive center" of the brain) is active during conscious decision-making. In this context, the individual observes the actions of others and attributes causes and motivation to those actions. When the individual concludes that the action is hostile, the neocortex gets to work hatching a response that will protect the individual's physical safety and/or social status through proactive aggression (Lochman et. al., p. 117). Think back to our look at Kahneman's "two systems" on page 26. Reactive aggression is the product of System 1: pure emotional response to a stimulus. Proactive aggression is the product of System 2, working to justify a System 1 emotional response to a stimulus, and then to plan and execute a response.

In both cases—reactive and proactive aggression—the key intervention for emotional management involves harnessing the teen's developing capacity for abstract thinking in order to get a handle on aggression. For teens unable to control their reactive aggression, that means developing basic anger management and impulse control skills. For teens with issues of proactive aggression, it means developing critical-thinking skills to help them more accurately assess other people's actions and motivations, and to craft healthier ways to get their emotional needs met.

Lessons 12–16 are designed to help students develop those skills. If you think your school needs a comprehensive curriculum to address this area, the Collaboration for Academic, Social, and Emotional Learning (CASEL) publishes an in-depth guide to evidence-based SEL curricula. You can find the guide at casel.org/guide.

Aggression Disorders

Unfortunately, some children's difficulties in regulating their emotions and aggression rise to the level where professional help is called for. The American Psychiatric Association's *Diagnostic and Statistical Manual 5* (DSM-5) identifies a set of disorders involving emotional and/or behavioral regulation. Here are some common aggression disorders found in DSM-5 (American Psychiatric Association, 2013).

OPPOSITIONAL DEFIANT DISORDER (ODD)

Diagnostic Features: "The essential feature of oppositional defiant disorder is a frequent and persistent pattern of angry/irritable mood, argumentative/defiant behavior, or vindictiveness . . . Individuals with this disorder typically do not regard themselves as angry, oppositional, or defiant. Instead, they often justify their behavior as a response to unreasonable demands or circumstances" (American Psychiatric Association, 2013, p. 463).

Prevalence: "Ranges from 1% to 11%, with an average prevalence estimate of around 3.3%" (ibid. p. 464).

CONDUCT DISORDER (CD)

Diagnostic Features: "The essential feature of conduct disorder is a repetitive and persistent pattern of behavior in which the basic rights of others or major age-appropriate societal norms and rules are violated . . . ." (ibid. p. 472).

Prevalence: "One-year prevalence estimates from 2% to more than 10%, with a median of 4%" (ibid. p. 473).

DISRUPTIVE MOOD DYSREGULATION DISORDER (DMDD)

Diagnostic Features: "The core feature of DMDD is chronic, severe, persistent irritability. This severe irritability [is accompanied by] frequent temper outbursts...[and] chronic, persistently irritable or angry mood that is present between the severe temper outbursts" (ibid. p. 156).

Prevalence: "The overall 6-month to 1-year prevalence of DMDD among children and adolescents probably falls in the 2%–5% range" (ibid. p. 157).

If you suspect that a student suffers one of these disorders, check to see if he or she has an Individualized Education Program (IEP) and, if so, whether they have been classified as Emotionally Disturbed (ED) and are getting appropriate mental health services. If not, consult with your school's counseling office to see if they agree that an assessment of the student is appropriate.

LESSON 12

What Sets You Off?

SEL Objectives: 5, 13, 14, 15, 16, 17

Preparing for the Lesson

Make copies of Worksheet 12: What Sets You Off? (page 110) and Worksheet 13: Chill (page 111).

Warm Up

Review with students four of the "five W's" of writing: *where, when, who,* and *what.*

Using the Activity

1. Distribute Worksheet 12. Have a volunteer read the instructions. Give students time to fill in the blanks. Make sure they understand that the purpose of the activity is to fill in "just the facts" about incidents in which they got angry. In addition to the Where? When? Who? What? sections, have students write in *how* they displayed their anger (such as yelling, slamming a door, shoving, and so on).

2. Note that the order of these sections is different from the traditional order of "who, what, where, when." The order used here goes from those elements that the student has most control over (the place and time where they have angry confrontation) to the element they have no control over (the other person's behavior). After students have filled in the blanks, lead a discussion of their work. Here are questions that will help them analyze their "anger situations":

Is there a pattern in what sets you off? Did you get angry two or more times at the same place or time? With the same person? With the same sort of behavior?

Very often, people with problems controlling their emotions discover that the same sorts of behavior (e.g., teasing) or the same people act as triggers. With young teens, certain locations are often "danger zones" for anger confrontations (e.g., the lunchroom, school bus, locker room). Making individuals mindful of the things that commonly set them off is a first step toward emotional management.

Sometimes managing our anger is as simple as consciously avoiding the situations that set us off. Or course, that's not always possible to do, but if a student *is* able to avoid confrontations, yet seeks them out anyway, it's important to make him conscious of that fact.

VALIDATING EMOTIONS

Is there such a thing as a "wrong" emotion?

Sure, you can fall in love with the wrong person. And we've all overreacted and thrown a fit over nothing. But even if it seems to be inappropriate or out of proportion to what's provoked it, *every emotion is real to the person who feels it.* Perhaps the least effective thing you can do when dealing with someone who is flipping out is to suggest that the person is over-reacting, or that he should just "get over it." Instead, the first step in helping someone get a handle on an overwhelming emotion is to *validate* the emotion. That means listening respectfully, and letting the upset person know that you understand why he or she feels that way.

Social & Emotional Learning © 2014 by Tom Conklin, Scholastic Teaching Resources

This is the key concept in emotional management. Grasping that they cannot control other people, but they can control themselves is a great challenge for many young teens, especially when they feel aggrieved by the other person. Individuals with problems managing reactive aggression find it difficult to control their response to others' behaviors. Those with problems managing proactive aggression believe that it is their right (and, often, duty!) to control how other people behave.

If you can't avoid the people or places that set you off, how can you deal with them without blowing up?

This is the point to hand out Worksheet 13, which presents basic anger management skills. Have volunteers read each of the steps out loud. Encourage students to share personal experiences in which they used each of the techniques. Discuss alternatives for some of the steps. For instance, instead of counting to ten, it's possible to distract yourself by silently singing "Happy Birthday." Counting backward from 100 can also work, in that it requires more concentration than counting to ten. If the situation is stable, angered individuals can build on their deep breathing by closing their eyes and visualizing a calming environment, such as a beach.

3. The suggestion "Don't react! *Respond*," is key. Discuss with students the difference between a reaction and a response. Elicit that a reaction is something you do without thinking, while a response is something that you say or do calmly and after careful thought.

4. Some young teens might still be concrete thinkers, and it can be helpful to give them a visual metaphor for anger. One I have found effective is an escalator: When we are getting angry, it's like we are on an up escalator. The trick is to jump over onto the down escalator. Instead of escalating our anger, *de*-escalate it!

Wrap Up

Discuss with students the fact that everyone gets angry. Tell them that it's important not to keep anger bottled up, and that talking about what makes them angry with a "safe" person is a good idea. Have students identify at least one safe person they can talk to after they get angry. The safe person could be a parent, sibling, friend, or caring adult such as a counselor or teacher—anyone they trust. Point out that the important thing is not trying immediately to solve whatever problems might be causing their anger. What matters is simply that they "vent" how they are feeling.

Extending the Lesson

Brainstorm with students their favorite ways to handle things when they get angry, such as playing video games, dancing, listening to music, playing sports. Have students find pictures of these activities in magazines or catalogs and create collages or a bulletin board called "How to Blow Off Steam."

Social Information Processing

ocial Information Processing (SIP) is what cognitive scientists call the way in which our minds make sense of other people's actions and motives and settle on our own response to those actions and motives. In terms used by young teens—SIP is what tells you how to act in all of life's "dramas."

This SIP model breaks down the different cognitive steps children go through as they process social interactions. It includes descriptions of how aggressive children may process each step (Crick & Dodge, 1994):

STEP 1 · READING SOCIAL CUES: Children use selective attention to take in social cues. This includes external cues (what other people do and say) and internal cues (their own memories of similar situations they have experienced in the past). *Aggressive children are more likely to focus selectively on hostile cues.*

STEP 2 · INTERPRETING THE CUES: Children figure out what motivates the social actions of other people, and themselves. *Aggressive children tend to see other people's actions as being more hostile than they really are, and to underestimate how hostile their own aggressive behavior is viewed by other people.*

STEP 3 · SELECTING A GOAL: After interpreting the social situation, children settle on a desired goal, such as staying out of trouble, getting even, or making a friend. *Aggressive children are more apt to select goals related to revenge, self-protection, or the desire to appear strong and dominant.*

STEP 4 · BRAINSTORMING RESPONSES: At this step, children consider different responses to the situation that can move them toward their goals. *Aggressive children are more prone to consider direct action over compromise or talking through problems.*

STEP 5 · PICKING A RESPONSE: After considering options, children pick a response. *An aggressive child's decision is often influenced by a belief that it's better to act forcefully than to stay passive.*

STEP 6 · ACTION!: This is the point when children will act out—physically and verbally. Note: If an aggressive child has decided on a nonaggressive reaction by, say, talking out a problem, it's very possible that his tone or body language will still be perceived as aggressive and, therefore, draw a hostile response. *This in turn can reinforce his belief that hostility and aggression are inevitable.*

It's important to recognize that in "real time" these steps can take place in a blink of the eye. Cognitive scientists theorize that these steps can occur in a nonlinear process, with some of the steps occurring simultaneously.

It's also important to note that, most aggressive children do not have difficulty in all of the six steps, but they may consistently act aggressively in one of the steps. For instance, if a teen consistently assumes in step 2 that other people disrespect him, it's important that he recognize this and work on developing the ability to consider other interpretations of people's actions. Therapists of the cognitive-behavioral school call these "automatic thoughts," and say they are the root cause of depression, anxiety, and other common mental health concerns. (See page 89.)

How can you make teens mindful of the SIP steps? It's a relatively abstract model and can be difficult for middle-school-aged children to grasp and connect with their own behavior. However, it is possible to take them "outside of their own heads" to do some experiential learning regarding the steps. How? With improvisational role-playing.

LESSON 13

Making a Scene

SEL Objectives: 5, 6, 9, 10, 11, 13

Preparing for the Lesson

Make copies of Worksheet 14: Making a Scene (112), and Worksheet 15: I've Seen This One Before (113).

Gather index cards and write roles and scenes on them, one per card. Be creative! The important thing is to include roles with clear character traits, and scenarios with inherent conflict. Here are some you might try:

ROLES	SCENARIOS
• Parent	• Cutting in line at a coffee shop
• Too-cool-for-school teen	• In a dentist's waiting room
• Spoiled 10-year-old	• A crowded elevator breaks down
• Sickly grandparent	• Slow service in a restaurant
• Nervous Nellie	• Talking and texting at a movie
• Tough cop	• One donut, three people
• Professor	• A winning lottery ticket
• Rich businessperson	• Outside a tattoo parlor
• Soldier	• A job interview
• Baby	• First time at the gym

You also can include well-known characters from books you have read in class as roles for students to play. Put the cards with the roles in one paper bag or hat, put the scenario cards in another.

Warm Up

Have students give their own definition of the word *improvise.* (to make something up as you go along) Focus the discussion on improvisation as a type of theater (often comedy). How is improvisation different from other types of plays? Elicit that in improvisation the actors play scenes without using a script. Tell students they are going to improvise some scenes.

Using the Lesson

1. Share Worksheet 14 with students, explaining that the guidelines on the sheet will help them as they improvise scenes. Have volunteers read each guideline out loud, then briefly discuss what it means.

2. Allow students to work in groups of three to four. Have groups take turns improvising scenes for the rest of the class. As a group takes its turn, the members each take a card from the collection of roles. Explain that this is the part they will play in the scene. Once everyone in the group has a role, have one member pick a scenario card. Before they begin the improvisation, tell students that they should do their best to make the scene last as long as possible. This means they have to work together and pay attention to each other in order to have the scene continue to build. Point out the importance of guidelines 4 and 5. If actors say "no" or otherwise try to control the scene all by themselves, the scene will quickly grind to a halt.

3. After each scene, ask members of the audience if they could tell what each actor's goal in the scene had been. Ask the actors if their attitudes or goals changed as they played out the scene. How? Did some of them get into the scene so much that they actually began to feel emotions? What emotions did they feel? Did that change the way they played the scene? Did it change their goals in the scene?

Wrap Up

After the groups have all had a chance to play a scene, connect the activity to the students' real life "scenes." Ask students if, in real life, they have "scripts" that they follow. Are there any dramas they play out over and over again? (e.g., recurring fights with siblings or peers) Challenge students to "change the script" for those real-life dramas. How can they improvise new ways to avoid the dramas and give them better endings? For example, maybe they can adjust their own goals or expectations, reinterpret the other person's motives or goals, or "be in the moment" and not jump to conclusions about what other people are up to.

Extending the Lesson

Use Worksheet 15: I've Seen This One Before as a writing exercise for students to reflect on any recurring conflicts in their lives.

Social & Emotional Learning © 2014 by Tom Conklin, Scholastic Teaching Resources

Communication Skills

I f you've been looking at the SEL Objectives covered in this book, you know that "communication" has been a recurring theme. Now let's look at communication as a topic in its own right. These activities are designed to make teens more mindful of their nonverbal communication; aware of the differences among assertive, passive, aggressive, and passive-aggressive communication styles; and to give them practice using communication skills in conflict resolution.

The following scenario is an example of classic nonverbal communication:

> *Two students—Adam and CJ—are huddled together in the back of the room. Adam is hunched over, staring into his lap, his hands under his desk's top. CJ peers over Adam's shoulder, his body trembling as he tries to hold in his laughter.*
>
> *"What's going on, fellas?" the teacher asks.*
>
> *Immediately, both boys sit up ramrod straight, innocent looks on their faces. "Nothing," Adam says.*

Yeah. Right.

Anyone who spends time supervising young teens quickly learns to read their body language—or risk anarchy! Fortunately, many young teens are as easy to read as an open book; they wear their emotions and attitudes on their sleeves. And it's not just teens. The fact is, when it comes to emotions, most human communication is nonverbal.

Landmark studies by psychologist Albert Mehrabian found just what percentages of communication are verbal and nonverbal. According to Mehrabian, when it comes to conveying our emotions and attitudes, 55 percent of communication is via our body language, 38 percent is our tone of voice, and only 7 percent is through words being spoken (Mehrabian & Ferris, 1968). Body language and vocal tone are especially significant when they are inconsistent with the words a person says. For instance, in the scenario above, Adam's words innocently claim that nothing is going on, but his body language says the opposite loud and clear.

How do we learn to "read" other people? Infants in the first weeks of life are able to express primary emotions such as joy, sadness, or fear. By the time they are 12 to 24 months old, children exhibit self-conscious emotions, such as embarrassment and pride, which involve responding to other people's emotions (Santrock, 2012, p. 304). Our skill at reading emotions improves with time and with our familiarity with the other persons involved. For instance, you will be better at reading the emotional state of a close family member than any highly trained professional psychologist would be, simply because of your shared experiences.

That being said, it is possible to increase one's sensitivity to body language and vocal tone, and to be more mindful of the signals you are putting out. As educators working with sensitive teens, it's important to be aware not only of what our students communicate nonverbally, but also of the signals we send out to them.

LESSON 14

Nonverbal Communication

SEL Objectives: 7, 9, 10

Preparing for the Lesson

Making teens mindful of nonverbal communication is an important aspect of developing their emotional and social management skills. Fortunately, their obsession with texting and social media—all exclusively verbal forms of communication— offers an excellent context for considering the piece missing from verbal communication: emotion.

Make copies of Worksheet 16: Emojis (page 114). Gather colored markers or pencils. Also, make copies of Worksheet 17: Nonverbal Scorecard (page 115) if you choose to use the lesson extension.

Warm Up

Ask students if they ever send text messages or use social media. Invite them to share any experiences in which they have misunderstood or been misunderstood while texting or using social networking. What caused the misunderstanding? Most

---

THE THREE C'S

Experts in the field refer to the "three c's" of accurate nonverbal communication: context, clusters, and consistency (Pease, 1981).

Context: This is step 1 of the SIP model, "Social Cues" (see page 68): Where are you and the other person, and what brings you there? Are you strangers standing in line at the store? A young couple on their first date? A mother confronting a daughter who has come home past curfew?

Clusters: As you take in the other person's social cues, look for "clusters" of behavior. Don't read too much into a single gesture or expression (unless it's a culturally accepted signifier, such as a thumbs up or a middle finger). For instance, just because the person you are with crosses her arms, don't automatically assume she is "closed off." It could be that she's simply feeling a chill. On the other hand, if the room is warm, and her folded arms are accompanied by a lack of eye contact and a deep sigh, that's a cluster of significant social cues.

Consistency: Do all of the social cues add up? Does the nonverbal behavior, tone of voice, and the meaning of spoken words all convey a consistent message? The lack of consistency between verbal and nonverbal communication can be very significant with young teens.

---

miscommunication when texting happens when people misinterpret the *intent* of a message—for instance, taking seriously a comment made as a joke.

Next, ask students to define *verbal communication*. Odds are, they will identify it with speaking. Ask them if texting and social media are forms of verbal communication. (Yes, because verbal communication refers to forms of communication based on words.) Bring up *nonverbal communication*, and ask how it is different from verbal communication. Elicit that nonverbal communication involves facial expression, body language, tone of voice, and so on. Discuss what sorts of things are communicated by nonverbal communication, such as your mood and attitude. Ask what communicates more to other people about how you are feeling, verbal or nonverbal communication? After discussing this, write Mehrabian's findings on the board: When it comes to emotions, feelings, and attitudes:

- 55 percent of communication is from body language

- 38 percent is tone of voice

- 7 percent is communicated in words

Ask how people communicate their moods and emotions via texting or social media. One answer: emojis.

Using the Lesson

1. Your students are apt to be familiar already with emojis—those colorful little images of smiley faces, stars, thumbs-up, and more—which let texters and social media users wordlessly share how they feel. Emojis were developed to appeal to Japanese kids more than a decade ago, and they have since caught on in the United States.

2. Tell students that their challenge is to improve on those emojis by creating their own that use facial expressions, body language, and tone. Distribute Worksheet 16 and make the color markers or pencils available.

3. Have a volunteer read the worksheet's instructions out loud. Tell students that in making their emojis, they can use stick figures in order to show body language, if they want. Also, students should use the color markers or pencils to convey the tone of the emoji. What words do you associate with the color red? (*hot, intense, fierce*) The color blue? (*cool, calm, sad*) Green? (*fresh, new; queasy, sick*)

4. Have students come up with their own moods, attitudes, or emotions that need an emoji, then draw them on the back of the sheet.

5. As students finish up their work, invite volunteers to draw their best emojis on the board without revealing what mood or emotion it's meant to represent. Let other students guess what each emoji stands for. Analyze each one, pointing out the elements that communicate the meaning of the emojis: facial expression, tone/color, body language, and so on.

Wrap Up

Point out that emojis are recognizable because they are based on how we interact with others in real life. Discuss the difference between emojis used while texting and nonverbal communication during face-to-face interactions (you must always *choose* to use an emoji, while body language and tone often communicate emotions without our being aware of it.)

Brainstorm a list of expressions/body language/tone that people use without being aware:

- Frowning
- Rolling eyes
- Hands on hips
- Pointing/jabbing finger

- Smiling
- Crossing arms/legs
- Nodding/shaking head
- Rocking back and forth

Extending the Lesson

Distribute Worksheet 17. It presents six different categories of nonverbal communication. Assign as homework that students use the scorecard as they watch television to record examples of nonverbal communication they see in a favorite program. (Suggest that students with DVRs at home freeze the images of the show in order to write descriptions of what they see without missing any of the show.) Challenge students to find at least one good example of each category of nonverbal communication and to describe it as precisely as possible, including the mood, emotion, or attitude that the character is showing through nonverbal communication. Here are some suggestions for each category:

Facial expression: smile, frown, scowl, sneer, furrowed brow

Body language: crossed arms or legs, slouching, hands on hips

Personal space: leaning in or back, standing too close

Eye gaze: staring, looking away, rolling eyes, winking

Touch: shaking hands, arms on shoulders, hugging, hitting

Appearance: clothes, hairstyle, grooming

Alternatively, you can use this as an in-class assignment using computers with an Internet connection. Students can use online video resources to find TV shows, movie clips, or appropriate music videos as source material for the assignment. Old silent films offer a good resource for analyzing nonverbal communication, as the actors silently convey a wide and nuanced variety of emotions and moods.

Social & Emotional Learning © 2014 by Tom Conklin, Scholastic Teaching Resources

Styles of Communication: Assertive, Passive, Aggressive, Passive-Aggressive

In our look at the limbic system and aggression (page 63), we saw that our brains are "hardwired" to respond to danger, and that the three basic responses to a threat are fight, flight, and freeze. Those three categories of response also crop up in the way we communicate during difficult or challenging social situations. A common way of identifying the styles is to label them as aggressive, passive-aggressive, and passive. You've seen the styles in action, no doubt, as different teens show different attitudes:

- The fighter, who aggressively states exactly what she wants, won't back down, and doesn't want to listen to any other points of view.

- The "flee-er," who avoids direct confrontation, but slyly lets everyone know how he feels through such passive-aggressive means as sarcasm, jokes, and procrastination.

- The "freezer," who passively goes along with the crowd and never "pushes back."

While not every young teen communicates exclusively in one of these styles, we all tend to have a fallback communication style, which is the result of a combination of factors, including temperament and life experiences. It's clear, though, that even if these styles are common and the predictable results of one's genetics and environment, they are often not the best modes of communication. Research indicates that young teens who habitually have social interactions that are overly aggressive or passive are at higher risk of developing mental health problems such as depression (Seligman, 1995, p. 261). Fortunately, there's a fourth communication style that finds the healthy middle ground between picking fights and rolling over: *assertiveness*.

One definition of assertiveness describes it as the ability to express one's rights and opinions while still respecting the rights of others (Wise, Bundy, Bundy, and Wise, 1991). An assertive teen combines the positive aspects of both aggression and passivity—a desire to be heard along with a desire not to hurt others—while avoiding the pitfalls of those communication styles. The way I describe it to young teens is to say that if you're assertive, you can stand up for yourself without stepping on anyone else's toes. And, just as life experiences can cause someone to develop an aggressive, passive, or passive-aggressive communication style, it's also possible to proactively develop assertiveness skills.

Lessons 15 and 16 focus on the assertive, passive, aggressive, and passive-aggressive attitudes. The first lesson presents the concepts and has students identify them using material from the novel *The Outsiders*. The second focuses on assertiveness in terms of conflict resolution and negotiation, arenas in which assertiveness skills really matter.

LESSON 15

Assertive, Passive, Aggressive, Passive-Aggressive

SEL Objectives: 1, 3, 5, 9, 10, 12, 16

Preparing for the Lesson

This lesson works well as a supplement to teaching the novel *The Outsiders*, although it can stand alone for use with students unfamiliar with the book. You can also use it in conjunction with the movie version of the story.

Make copies of Worksheet 18: What's Their Attitude? (pages 116 and 117). (Note that it is in two parts.)

Warm Up

Ask students what it means to "have an attitude." How do you know when someone has an attitude? (Because of how they act.) Discuss how people communicate their attitude to others. If you have reviewed verbal and nonverbal communication (page 72), refer back to that discussion. How do people communicate an attitude in words? In their tone of voice? In how they act? Point out that we often say that someone "has an attitude" as shorthand for the fact that the person has a bad attitude. How do people communicate that they have a *good* attitude? Tell students you are going to explore a way to classify different types of attitude.

Using the Lesson

1. Distribute Part I of the worksheet. Have volunteers read each of the four types of attitude described. Discuss each type, focusing on the way people in each of these categories communicate their attitude—including verbal and nonverbal communication. Discuss whether or not people always have the same sort of attitude. What can cause someone's attitude to change? List the causes on the board. Make sure the list includes the following:

   • Your mood (*happy, sad, scared*, and so on)

   • How you feel physically (*sick, tired, hungry*, and so on)

   • The situation (*Are you in class? The lunchroom? At a baseball game? Church?*)

   • The people you are with (*Are they assertive? Passive? Aggressive? Passive-aggressive?*)

2. Focus on what it means to have an assertive attitude. Discuss what it takes to be assertive. Share the following qualities of assertive communication:

   • Clearly state what you think, feel, and want.

   • Listen respectfully to other people.

   • Let other people know that you hear them.

   • Control your anger. Let people know if you are angry without "flipping out."

3. Have students work on their own to fill in the blanks on the bottom of the worksheet to identify characters' attitudes. (Answers: Ponyboy—assertive; Cherry—passive-aggressive; Dally—aggressive; Johnny—passive) If you are using this in conjunction with the book, or if students are familiar with the book, have them discuss examples of the characters' actions that express these attitudes. Do the characters *always* show the same attitude? (No. For instance, Johnny performs the ultimate act of aggression by killing another boy who was holding Ponyboy's head under water.) Do the characters *usually* show the same attitude? (Yes, because they are basically consistent in how they react to other people.)

4. Distribute Part II of Worksheet 18. Have students work singly or in small groups to determine which attitude is being displayed in each excerpt. These quotes are open to interpretation, but students should be able to give reasons for the attitude they describe. Possible answers:

1. Assertive. Ponyboy clearly states how he feels. Although he doesn't like Cherry's attitude and lets her know he is angry, he is not attacking her. He shares with her the reasons why he is angry.

2. Aggressive. Ponyboy verbally and physically lashes out at the Socs. Although he is provoked (as readers of the book will know), his actions escalate the hostile situation.

3. Assertive. Ponyboy says that the only reason to fight is for self-defense, whereas his friends will fight for fun and pride. (Point out that Ponyboy hangs out with aggressive kids, which raises the likelihood that he will be put into situations where he will have to defend himself.)

4. Passive-aggressive. Cherry claims that she and her friends don't feel emotions, and that "nothing is real" for them, and this makes them "sophisticated." She insults Ponyboy while pretending to compliment him.

5. Aggressive. (This one is complex.) Ponyboy basically says that he will fight for his friends whether they are right or wrong. Or, **Assertive.** Ponyboy clearly states what he feels and why.

Wrap Up

Ask students about their own attitudes and the attitudes of people that they know. Which attitude is easiest to get along with? Which is the most difficult to cope with? Which one do they admire most?

Extending the Lesson

Challenge students to name characters from other books who provide examples of each of the four attitudes. Have them write brief descriptions of each character, giving examples of the attitude in each of the characters' actions.

LESSON 16

Conflict Resolution

SEL Objectives: 5, 6, 8, 9, 10, 11, 13, 17

Conflict resolution is a very large topic, with entire curricula devoted to it. Here, we focus on conflict resolution in terms of communication skills and link it to the four communication styles (or "attitudes") presented in the previous lesson.

Preparing for the Lesson

Make copies of Worksheet 19: Conflict Resolution (pages 118 and 119). (Note that it is in two parts.)

Warm Up

Briefly review the four attitudes presented in the previous lesson. Ask students how they think each one works when it comes to resolving conflicts. How does an aggressive person handle conflicts? A passive person? Passive-aggressive? Assertive?

Using the Lesson

1. Have a volunteer describe a recent disagreement he or she has had with a friend or family member. After the volunteer describes the disagreement, focus on its elements:

    • *Who* was involved in the conflict?

    • *What* did each person want?

    • *How* did the individuals in the conflict communicate what they wanted? (Did they yell? Give reasons for their position? Use sarcasm?) Identify which of the four attitudes they displayed.

    • *Was the conflict resolved*? If so, who "won" (if anyone)? How do you know?

2. Distribute Part I of Worksheet 19. Have volunteers read aloud each of the four attitudes and how they operate in a conflict. Ask students to focus on the possible outcomes. Which outcome is the best? Which one is the worst? Why? Encourage students to be honest. If a student is an "I win/You lose" sort of person, have the student explain why he thinks that is the best outcome.

3. Let students work in small groups of two to four to write responses to the questions at the bottom of the worksheet. As they work, make sure that they understand that the first question asks which attitude is best for resolving conflicts *so that they stay resolved*. When they are done responding to the questions, let different groups report their responses. Ask if other groups came to different conclusions and, if so, have them talk about their differences of opinion.

Social & Emotional Learning © 2014 by Tom Conklin, Scholastic Teaching Resources

Possible answers:

A. Assertive "I win/You win" is the best attitude for resolving a conflict so that it stays resolved, since no one is left with a motivation to keep fighting.

B. Aggressive "I win/You lose" is probably the hardest attitude to deal with, because if you're on the other end of it, you get nothing out of the conflict.

C. Assertive "I win/You win" is probably the hardest attitude to keep up, because you have to face the conflict (which is hard if you are passive), and you also have to give in a little (which is hard if you're aggressive).

4. Distribute Part II of the worksheet, which presents five scenarios describing typical conflicts involving young teens. Students should continue to work in their groups. Have them silently read through the scenarios, then pick two to work on. (Note: The conflicts are in roughly descending order, from most trivial and easiest to solve to most complex and difficult to resolve.)

5. Have students write a brief report for each of the conflicts they have chosen. The report should identify the following:

- Who is involved in each conflict

- What each person wants out of the conflict

- At least three possible outcomes for the conflict, with at least one of those outcomes being a "win/win"

- What obstacles could prevent a "win/win" solution (such as the attitudes of the people involved or the circumstances surrounding the problem)

Wrap Up

Have each group report their win/win solutions. If there is more than one win/win for any of the scenarios, discuss which one would be most satisfying or easiest to achieve.

Extending the Lesson

Have students make posters to illustrate each of the four attitudes in conflict resolution. Challenge them to come up with slogans to encourage win/win solutions, with images to support that attitude.

Bullying

In the popular young adult novel *Thirteen Reasons Why*, Jay Asher recounts the harrowing story of Hannah Baker, a troubled teenager just starting out at a new school, where she soon becomes the subject of rumors and sexual gossip. Pretty and apparently popular, Hannah struggles with the social fallout of the rumors and innuendos, until the pain and anger of being targeted drives her to take her own life. Hannah's death is the direct result of bullying.

Bullying? Really? Hannah wasn't beaten up by tough kids. She was friendly, had a sense of humor, and attracted the attention of boys. Some of her peers spread rumors about her, true, but that's normal "teen stuff." After all, "sticks and stones" and all that, right?

Wrong.

Bullies come in all shapes and sizes—from the "classic bully," a physical aggressor tormenting his smaller peers, to the "psychological ninjas," kids whose agenda is to get peers to hurt themselves. It's relational aggression—the domain of those ninjas, in which teens isolate, insult, and humiliate each other—that might be the most dangerous type of bullying. (See the sidebar on page 83.) Let's take a closer look at bullying, in all of its forms.

According to social scientists, bullying is defined by three essential elements. It 1) is aggressive behavior; 2) occurs with frequency over an extended period of time; and 3) involves an imbalance of power between the aggressor and victim (Olweus, 1995). The number of bullying incidents in American schools is truly distressing. According to the latest National Center for Education Statistics (NCES) report on Indicators of School Crime and Safety, almost 30 percent of students in middle school and high school were bullied in 2012. Being the subject of rumors—the relational aggression dramatized in *Thirteen Reasons Why*—is the most common form of bullying. In 2011, one in four teenage girls were the subject of rumors, with 13 percent of boys so targeted. Verbal aggression was the next most common type of bullying, followed by physical bullying, with 9 percent of boys and 7 percent of girls saying that they had been shoved, tripped, or spit on (Robers, et. al., 2013, page 44).

Clearly, "traditional" physical bullying is a problem in middle schools. But relational and verbal aggression is more common, and girls are more frequently the targets of name-calling, insults, and rumors. This type of relational aggression has been greatly exacerbated by "cyber-bullying," which happens when rumors and taunting at school

WHEN BULLYING TURNS DEADLY

It's become a depressingly familiar story: A young person is hounded mercilessly by bullies, until the victim can take no more and ends his or her own life. Sometimes these cases become media sensations, especially when criminal prosecutions follow the deadly bullying. In her book *Sticks and Stones: Defeating the Culture of Bullying and Rediscovering the Power of Character and Empathy*, Emily Bazelon provides in-depth profiles of kids involved in deadly bullying situations. It's an excellent, thorough, and thought-provoking look at the bully phenomenon.

Social & Emotional Learning © 2014 by Tom Conklin, Scholastic Teaching Resources

spill over into social networking sites or text messages. Cyber-bullying can be far more hurtful than typical verbal aggression. The name-calling or false rumors that would otherwise be confined within the school walls can be laid out for hundreds of strangers to see—or, if it "goes viral," even more. According to the NCES report, about one in ten American teens report being targeted by cyber-bullies over the course of a school year, again, with girls more frequent targets than boys.

So who are bullies, and why do they choose to victimize their peers? A common way to think about the bullying dynamic is to see it in terms of bullies, victims, and bystanders:

BULLIES: Contrary to the popular stereotype, most bullies are not isolated "losers" tortured by low self-esteem. A typical bully, if anything, has better social skills than his peers. Social researchers use words like "sociable," "assertive," "good leaders," and "popular" to describe a typical middle school bully (Gasser & Keller, 2009). Of course, not every bully is a swaggering "alpha-kid." Social scientists also identify a class of school-yard aggressor they call *bully-victims*. A bully-victim is the target of bullies, who in turn acts aggressively toward others (ibid.). Both bullies and bully-victims use aggression to establish power and dominance, are generally hostile toward the school environment, and "get something" from their behavior—social prestige in the case of bullies, a sense of revenge for bully-victims.

VICTIMS: Most children targeted by bullies fall under the heading social scientists call *passive victims*. They are generally sensitive, quiet, and often suffer from low self-esteem. Experts also identify a second, far less common type of victim called *provocative victims*. These are the kids whose behaviors and attitudes rub other kids the wrong way. Often, these teens have temperaments and behaviors that also turn off teachers and other adults, which can obscure the fact that they're being targeted by bullies. Provocative victims often cross the line and become bully-victims in their own right.

BYSTANDERS: The relationship between a bully and his victim is clear, but it's the third element—an audience of bystanders—that holds the key to understanding the bullying phenomenon. As we've seen, a bully often targets someone not simply out of dislike for the victim, but also in order to gain status. And, all to often, that's just what they get. In one recent study, researchers conducted in-depth interviews with students at a Florida middle school, where they found that 70 percent of the students reported "enjoyable experiences" with school-based aggression. The kids reported being "energized" and "hyped" by aggression in school, and enjoyed reporting it to others after the fact (Kerbs & Jolley, 2007). Any anti-bullying intervention that focuses on bullies and victims without also addressing bystanders misses an essential piece of the puzzle.

To sum up what we know about bullying: It's a pattern of ongoing, aggressive behavior that involves an imbalance of power between the bully and his victim. The aggression can be either relational, verbal, or physical, or some combination of the three. Relational aggression is the most common kind of bullying, and girls are more often the victims of this kind of aggression. Finally, bullying is a "triangle," consisting of bullies, victims, and bystanders. Now, with all of this in mind, we can begin to explore the best way to address bullying.

Let's start by looking at three common anti-bullying approaches that do *not* work.

IGNORING THE PROBLEM: The most common adult response to bullying is to file it away as typical kid behavior, and to assume that learning to deal with a bully is an important life lesson. While this may be true when it comes to resolving conflicts between peers who are on an equal footing, bullying presents a special case. The bully-victim relationship is really an abuser-abused relationship, and the power differential between a bully and her victim makes it impossible for a victim to stand up for herself—not without support. Letting the abusive relationship fester is bad for both the bully and victim: Studies show that bullying victims are at greater risk for depression and anxiety, while bullies themselves grow to be adults more likely to commit crime and serve time behind bars (Olweus, 2011).

MEDIATION: Many anti-bullying programs include peer mediation or some other form of negotiated conflict resolution as essential elements. But, as we've seen, most bullies have social skills and are not afraid to be assertive, while their preferred victims have low self-esteem and introverted personalities. Under these circumstances, mediations or other negotiations can be ineffective or downright counterproductive, with socially competent bullies manipulating the process to meet their own needs. Too often, mediation between a bully and his victim becomes a school-sanctioned extension of the abusive relationship.

BLAMING THE VICTIM: No one cares to admit that they blame the victim when it comes to bullying. But that's exactly what we do when we counsel a victim not to cry or otherwise show the bully that her bullying hurts. A variation on this approach is to tell the victim to let the bully know how being bullied feels in the hopes of sparking an empathetic response. Look: a bully knows *exactly* how her victims feel, and to tell victims not to react to bullying is to make them responsible for the pain. Perhaps the most counterproductive blame-the-victim strategy is to advise a victim to "keep his head low" or otherwise to not draw attention to himself (Davis, 2009). Bullies target victims not because of what the victims do, but because of who the victims are. It's up to the bullies, not the victims, to alter their behaviors.

If these common responses to bullying are generally unsuccessful, what does work? Psychologist Dan Olweus is a pioneer in bullying studies, and has designed one of the most popular intervention programs (the Olweus Bullying Prevention Program, found at www.violencepreventionworks.org). According to Olweus, a successful anti-bullying program will be school-wide, addressing the entire school population. The goal is to create an "environment characterized by warmth, positive interest, and involvement from adults" combined with "firm limits to unacceptable behaviors." The essential components of such a program include (Olweus, 1995):

1. Awareness and involvement with all of the adults in the school

2. Good supervision in the lunchroom and other places where students socialize

3. Questionnaires or other instruments to assess student experiences with bullying

4. Clear and firm class rules against bullying, along with regular class discussions on the topic

5. "Serious talks" with bullies, victims, and their families

One necessary part of any successful program is consistency. Bullying exists in a social context, and to change bullying behavior it's necessary to change the context in which it thrives. That means any changes to rules, rewards, and punishments should be across the board and consistent.

Classroom teachers, acting alone, can only be responsible for component 4 above. Teachers can, however, be advocates for anti-bullying efforts in the school if administrators are neglecting the issue or are trying unsuccessful approaches. As a start, here are two classroom activities that can raise awareness of bullying and its effects.

WARNING SIGNS = TAKE ACTION

It's a fact: Bullying and teen suicidal behavior and ideation are linked. Studies indicate that while victims of bullies are most prone to suicidality, everyone involved in the "bullying triangle"—victims, bullies, and onlookers—are at greater risk of suicidal thinking and behavior (Kim & Leventhal, 2008; Rivers & Noret, 2010). It's important to recognize, though, that bullying is one of many risk factors in teen suicidality.

It's vital for educators to be sensitive to all warning signs of suicidality, which includes bullying behavior. According to the American Psychological Association, other warning signs of suicidal behavior include:

- Chronic sadness or depression
- Withdrawal from friends
- Losing interest in school and hobbies
- Drastic changes in behavior
- Talking or writing about death or suicide
- Increased risky behavior
- Losing interest in personal appearance or hygiene

If any you know student that appears to be at risk of suicide or self-harm, *take him or her very seriously!* Refer those troubled students to the school counseling staff, and follow up to make sure that the counselors address the situation. It's all too easy to dismiss suicidal behavior as mere "attention seeking" and to minimize it. Yes, such behavior is an attempt to get attention—and the only acceptable response is to pay attention, and get the suicidal individual the help he or she needs.

LESSON 17

Anti-Bullying Project

SEL Objectives: 6, 7, 8, 9, 10, 11, 14, 15, 16,17

As suggested by Olweus and other researchers, an effective anti-bullying program is a school-wide effort. You and your students can do your part by making a school-wide anti-bullying public awareness campaign. Tailor your efforts to dovetail with your school's existing anti-bullying efforts, or make your students' campaign a tool for raising awareness of the issue for both students and staff.

Preparing for the Lesson

This is a multipart lesson consisting of three phases:

- Research
- Creative work
- Putting the campaign into action

You can have students work in three groups, with each group responsible for one of the above parts of the campaign. This activity presents an excellent opportunity for students to focus on teamwork and cooperative learning.

Make copies of Worksheets 20, 21, and 22 (pages 120–122) for use by your research team. You can save paper by having students make a master sheet to record responses to their surveys using tally marks. (Note: Point out to students that there is no "name" line on these surveys to allow responders to remain anonymous.)

Warm Up

Let students know they are going to be planning and sharing a public awareness campaign on the subject of bullying. Discuss with students other public awareness campaigns they may be familiar with (such as anti-smoking, drunk-driving awareness, or anti-obesity campaigns).

Using the Lesson

1. Brainstorm with students what makes a public awareness campaign successful. Point out that effective campaigns have a clear, simple message and present that message in memorable ways. Also point out that successful campaigns are based on research, and use statistics to back up their messages. Tell students that their anti-bullying campaign will be made by three different working groups: a research team, a creative team, and an action team to put the campaign out into the public.

2. Tell students that the campaign will take place in three stages, with one group taking charge in each of the stages.

3. In the first phase, students conduct school-wide research on people's experiences with bullying and their attitudes about bullies. Students also plan the other parts of the campaign. Research should be conducted with three different populations: Students, adults in the school, and parents.

PHASE ONE: RESEARCH (2–4 DAYS)

Research Team: See Worksheets 20, 21, and 22 for possible approaches to research surveys for each of the three target populations. Students can use these survey questionnaires, or adapt them to include questions of their own. The point of the research is to find out how each target group has experienced bullying, and to learn what works and doesn't work when it comes to bullying prevention.

Members of the research team can conduct surveys and supervise members of the other working groups in taking surveys. Surveys of students and school personnel can take place during lunch hours and at the beginning and end of the school day. School personnel includes any adult who works at the school, including teachers, administrators, lunchroom workers, bus drivers, and custodians. Parent surveys can be taken home by each student in the class, and also used by members of the research team to survey parents at school sporting events or other extracurricular activities.

Creative Team: As the research team conducts research, members of the creative team brainstorm possible themes and slogans for the campaign, and plan what media they will use to convey their messages (posters, videos, songs, school announcements).

Action Team: Members of the action team help the research team to survey the school and parents. Other members of the action team should work with the creative team to plan how the creative team's ideas will be executed. This could entail getting materials for posters, getting access to needed A/V equipment, and contacting the school office or other authorities about permission needed to put the different parts of the campaign into action.

4. In the second phase, members of the creative team make the materials to convey their anti-bullying message, supported by the research team's findings and with the help of the action team.

PHASE TWO: CREATIVE (2–3 DAYS)

Creative Team: This team coordinates the efforts to make anti-bullying posters, videos, audiorecordings, school announcement scripts, and whatever other media they have chosen. Again, make sure that they are conveying a clear and consistent message in their materials.

Research Team: Members of this team compile the results of their surveys. Encourage them to express their finds using statistics, such as "X out of X students say the most effective way to stop bullying is . . ." If they use the surveys provided in this book, make sure that they compare results between students, school personnel, and parents—especially on the question of how serious each group thinks the bullying problem is. Have students look to see if students and adults agree on the seriousness of the issue, or if any of the groups think bullying is more serious than the other groups.

The research team should work closely with the creative team to make sure that their findings are part of the campaign's message.

Action Team: Members of this team work with the creative team to create the campaign's posters, videos, and other media messages.

5. In the third phase, students blanket the school with their anti-bullying campaign.

PHASE THREE: ACTION (1+ DAYS)

Action Team: This team coordinates efforts to put up posters, make public service announcements, post videos, and execute all other parts of the campaign.

Creative Team and Research Team: Those members of these teams not helping the action team should work together to make a final report of the research team's work. The report should include the campaign's slogans and themes. Make enough copies of the report to share with other teachers, school administrators, and local media (newspapers, local TV news, and so on).

CROSSING THE LINE

Perspective taking is defined as "the ability to assume other people's perspectives and understand their thoughts and feelings" (Santrock, 2012, p. 342). It's an important SEL skill students use to resist and squelch bullying behavior. Bystanders who egg on a bully and gossip about his behavior are already engaged in perspective taking. The problem is, they identify with the bully, not his victim. In my experience, this is often because bystanders think the victim deserves to be bullied. This can happen because, in the kids' eyes, the victim overreacts to the bully's initial aggression, which is usually characterized as "kidding" or "goofing around." The victim's reaction often entails letting adults know about the bullying, which qualifies as "snitching" and invites further attack. The key is to help bystanders understand that there is nothing funny about a bully's calculated cruelty, and that one person's "joke" can cross the line and become someone else's cruel, hurtful attack.

Social & Emotional Learning © 2014 by Tom Conklin, Scholastic Teaching Resources

Wrap Up

After students have planned and created their public awareness campaign, discuss what surprised them most about the experience. Was it people's attitudes about bullying? What sort of anti-bullying actions students said work best? The school's reactions to the campaign? Talk about what worked best in the campaign, and what they would do differently next time.

Extending the Lesson

A month or so after the anti-bullying campaign was launched, have members of the research team try to discover if it has had an effect. Suggest the following methods:

- Ask the school administration if there has been a change in reported bullying incidents

- Redo the surveys to see if student attitudes about bullying have changed

- Survey students to find if they have experienced or witnessed more or fewer bullying incidents than previously

Stress

"For there is nothing either good or bad, but thinking makes it so."

FROM *Hamlet*, Act II, Scene ii, William Shakespeare

Stress. We've all felt it. Whether it's the pressure of a deadline, financial insecurity, illness, or something as silly as being stuck in traffic when you're running late, everyone has had that overwhelming sensation that life is throwing up more challenges than they can handle.

Stress can be especially difficult for young teens. Think of what an eighth grader faces: the physical stressors of puberty, the complex social byways of middle school, a changing relationship with parents and other family members—not to mention algebra! It's no wonder, then, that the inability to cope with stress has been linked to many problems facing teens, including "poor academic performance, conduct problems, anxiety, depression, suicide, eating disorders, and violence" (Kovacs, 1997). Hopefully, many of the activities throughout these pages can help middle schoolers to handle the stress caused by their developing sense of self and challenging relationships. For now, let's look at coping skills specifically designed for handling stress in any situation, from test-taking to dealing with rejection.

The two coping skill strategies that follow are adapted from cognitive behavioral therapy (CBT) models. CBT was developed by psychologists from the 1960s through the 1980s, and is most closely associated with psychologists Aaron Beck and Albert

When Stress Is All Too Real

Teens living in extreme conditions of poverty and abuse are at special risk of stress-related problems. As we've seen, our nervous system has evolved to respond to danger through an automatic "fight or flight" response. When it's activated, the flight-or-flight response system releases stress hormones and other powerful chemicals in the body. Youngsters in stressful environments have their flight-or-flight systems constantly overstimulated. The result? "Research shows that repeated exposure to stressful situations such as neglect, child abuse, and poverty can stunt brain growth, leading to persistent negative effects on mental functions later in life, as well as an increased risk of mental health problems" (Costandi, 2013, p. 140). Teens in such harsh environments probably will require special services outside of the classroom to help them cope with their stress.

If you suspect that any student is suffering from clinical anxiety or depression, or is the victim of neglect or abuse, have that student screened by an appropriate counselor. In the meantime, most young teens will benefit from understanding and using the basic concepts presented here.

Ellis. If CBT itself is of fairly recent vintage, the ideas behind its approach go back thousands of years, and are neatly summed up in the quote from *Hamlet* that opened this section. Simply put, CBT holds that our moods and emotions—happiness, sadness, fear, love—are the result of our conscious minds interpreting and appraising ourselves and our environment. Thus, if you are stuck in a negative mood, the challenge is to "reframe" the way you think about the situation that is causing your mood. As Hamlet so memorably said, "good" and "bad" are interpretations, not inherent qualities. And those interpretations affect our emotions and moods.

Here are two CBT activities that can start students to develop the skills to get a handle on stress.

LESSON 18

Self-Spin

SEL Objectives: 1, 2, 3, 4

Earlier, we looked at "automatic thoughts"—those deep-seated, knee-jerk responses we have to different social situations. Psychologists say that our automatic thoughts are often based on mental schemas—fundamental cognitions that we develop in our earliest years (Young, Klosko, and Weishar, 2003). Automatic thoughts are linked to a variety of emotional health problems, including conditions such as anxiety, depression, aggression, and personality disorders. The early adolescent years are a critical period for addressing this issue, for it's as we make the transition to Piaget's formal operations stage—purely abstract reasoning—that those schemas we formed as toddlers can "harden" into inflexible patterns of thought. Middle school is a prime time for youngsters to begin to challenge their automatic thoughts.

CBT psychologists have identified and classified a variety of negative automatic thoughts, technically known as "cognitive distortions." Worksheet 23 lists nine of the most common cognitive distortions, as identified by David Burns, one of the most influential CBT practitioners (Burns, 1980, pp. 42–43). I have rewritten Burns's cognitive distortions into "teen friendly" terms, which I call "self-spin."

Preparing for the Lesson
Make copies of Worksheet 23: Self-Spin (page 123).

Warm Up
Ask students what it means to "spin" something. Give this example:

> *You want to spend Saturday hanging out with friends. Your parents want you to study for the coming state achievement tests. How can you "spin" the situation so that your parents might think it's a good idea for you to visit your friends?*

Allow students to brainstorm ways to spin that situation so that their parents will see things their way. (Possible answer: You want to study with your friends.) Point out that spin is not an out-and-out lie. It's a way of presenting a situation so that other people see it the way you want them to see it. Ask students if we ever "spin" ourselves?

Using the Lesson

1. Distribute Worksheet 23. Have a student read the title and introduction of the worksheet, then pause to discuss it. Point out that what they are about to read are examples of negative spin, not positive. Make sure students understand that the self-spin thoughts here are things we think without being aware of it. You can describe them as "automatic thoughts."

2. Have volunteers read each of the nine self-spin examples. Stop after each one and ask if anyone in the class ever thinks in the way described. After all nine types of self-spin have been described, invite volunteers to describe an incident in which they used one of the forms of self-spin.

3. Have students work in groups of three. Challenge each group to write a short skit with three characters in a common setting (such as in the lunchroom, at the mall, hanging out at home and watching TV). Tell students that in the skit, all three characters must come to agreement on something (picking a game to play, a store to visit, a TV show to watch, and so on). The trick is, each character always self-spins using one of the nine examples shown on the worksheet.

4. When students have written their brief skit, let them take turns performing them for each other. Have those in the audience guess which of the nine self-spins each character kept using.

Wrap Up

Discuss how it felt to play the different characters, and how it feels in real life to have these sorts of automatic thoughts. Go over each of the nine self-spins. Ask if they are ever accurate. For instance, are things always black and white? Does one bad thing spoil everything around it? Point out that these self-spins are most often not accurate, and they make you feel bad. What's the best way to counteract them?

Extending the Lesson

This lesson works most effectively in conjunction with the next lesson, Need a Coping Skill? It's as Easy as A-B-C.

LESSON 19

Need a Coping Skill? It's as Easy as A-B-C

SEL Objectives: 1, 2, 3, 4, 5, 6, 14, 16

Preparing for the Lesson

This lesson uses a basic problem-solving heuristic to help students challenge the sorts of negative automatic thoughts presented in Lesson 18: Self-Spin. This simple model was developed and expanded upon by Dr. Albert Ellis (Ellis & Harper, 1997). I've presented the bare bones of the concept in a way that is accessible to young teens.

Make copies of Worksheet 24: Need a Coping Skill? It's as Easy as A-B-C (page 124).

Warm Up

Write the word *adversity* on the board and ask students what it means. (Possible answer: when something bad happens.) Discuss how facing adversity makes you feel. If no student brings it up, mention that adversity causes you to feel stress.

Point out that another way to think about adversities is to view them as challenges: Adversity can describe things as varied as a tough homework assignment, an illness, or a fight with a friend. Ask their opinions on what is the most important thing for a person to do when it comes to coping with adversity and the stress it can cause.

Using the Lesson

1. Distribute Worksheet 24. Go over the A-B-C model presented on the worksheet. Point out that many people see this as an A-C model. That is, when they face adversity (A), they jump right to a negative response (C). The most important step in this model is B, or beliefs about the adverse situation and our ability to cope with it.

2. In the example presented, the adversity is a challenging math test. The belief is "I can't do this!" This kind of thinking leads to the consequences: little or no studying, lots of stress and panic, and a poor grade. Make sure students understand that it's not possible to change the A, and to change the C from negative to positive they first have to change B—their belief about the adversity and their ability to handle it.

3. Work as a class to fill in the next A-B-C form on the worksheet. Brainstorm a difficult situation to put in the A slot. Steer the students to pick a situation pertaining to social interactions. Example:

   A stands for
   Adversity
   Boyfriend/girlfriend says, "Let's just be friends."

4. Come up with a negative interpretation of the event to put in the B slot. Example:

> B stands for
> Belief
> "It's because I'm ugly and stupid."

5. Next, identify the consequence of the adversity and negative belief about it. Example:

> C stands for
> Consequences
> Sadness, loss of confidence.

FLOW

Athletes, artists, and musicians all experience it. There are different ways to describe it: *"In the zone." "Feeling it." "In the groove."* Psychologists have a word for it, too: *Flow.*

Flow is that sensation you get when you are doing something that you love, the activity is a challenge, and your skills are perfectly honed to meet that challenge. Psychologist Mihaly Csikszentmihalyi developed the concept and definition of flow, and identified characteristics of the flow state, including (Csikszentmihalyi, 2009):

- Intense focus on what you're doing as you do it
- Losing your self-consciousness
- Having a strong sense of control
- Time flies
- The activity is its own reward

A flow activity is a great way to manage stress. In fact, many middle school students instinctively latch on to flow activities. Mastering a video game, for example, puts the gamer into a flow state. The challenge for educators is to help young teens find the most constructive ways to achieve flow. Possible flow activities include the following:

- Snowboarding
- Dancing
- Yoga
- Building models
- Cooking
- Creative writing

6. Finally, brainstorm positive beliefs that could take the place for the negatives in the B slot, and how it affects the C consequences. Example:

B stands for	C stands for
Belief	Consequences
"We do need some time apart."	Hope for the future.

Have students work in groups of two to four to come up with other situations, beliefs, and consequences to put into the A-B-C slots. Tell them to start with negative beliefs for slot B. Then have them change the belief in the B slot to something positive, and identify the consequences of that. Students can refer to the Self-Spin examples on Worksheet 23 for suggestions of negative attitudes to apply to their situations.

Wrap Up

Have each group of students share one of their A-B-C sequences with negative beliefs and consequences. Let other students in the class brainstorm alternative positive beliefs and the resulting consequences, then have the original team share their positive beliefs and consequences. As the different groups share their work, discuss how many different possible positive beliefs there are for each of the adverse situations.

Extending the Lesson

Brainstorm with students other positive ways to cope with stress:

- Exercise
- Write a poem
- Sing
- Plan your dream vacation
- Clean your room
- Eat nutritious foods
- Smile
- Listen to music
- Paint or draw
- Dance
- Read a favorite book
- Watch a funny TV show
- Do a random act of kindness

Addiction

As we've seen, young teens are susceptible to stress and need coping strategies for managing it. Unfortunately, too many teens settle on unhealthy ways of managing their stress. Substance abuse is probably the most dangerous and self-defeating way teens have of trying to cope with their daily cares.

What drives teens to use dangerous mind-altering substances? Peer pressure is a major factor. Studies indicate that teen substance use—so often seen by teens themselves as an act of rebellion and independence—is actually driven by a teen's desire to conform. For instance, one study demonstrates that teen boys drink alcohol to increase their popularity, and "keeping up" with peers is a major factor in underage intoxication (Balsa, Homer, French, and Norton, 2010).

Another significant contributing factor is parental attitudes toward substance use. The National Center on Substance Abuse (CASA) has conducted research and found that teens who say their parents do not strongly object to the teens' use of substances are far more likely to use drugs and alcohol. In fact, those kids with lax parents are ten times more likely to get drunk than are their peers, and eight-and-a-half times more likely to use marijuana (The National Center on Addiction and Substance Abuse at Columbia University, 2012). In my own clinical experience, teen substance users almost inevitably have a family history of substance abuse or addiction.

Finally, as I mention above, stress is a major contributing factor for use. The CASA study found that teens reporting high stress are three times likelier to use marijuana, twice as likely to use alcohol, and almost twice as likely to smoke cigarettes as their less-stressed peers (ibid.).

How can educators help students avoid the dangers of substance abuse and addiction? Unfortunately, despite decades of drug-abuse prevention efforts in the schools, there is little research that points to clearly successful, evidence-based approaches. In fact, one clear and consistent research finding is that the most popular substance-abuse prevention program, D.A.R.E., does *not* work (Vincus, Ringwalt, Harris, and Shamblen, 2010; Rosenbaum, 2007). Research does, however, point to some characteristics of successful programs:

Early intervention: When it occurs in elementary grades and middle school, early intervention is linked to lower rates of substance use by teens (Spoth, R., et. al., 2013; Jackson, C., et. al., 2011).

Broad scope: Successful programs address substance use and abuse "across domains"—instruction isn't limited to one setting (such as the classroom) and addresses the topic in the context of the school, home, and social environments (Jackson, C., et. al., ibid.).

Interactivity: The most effective programs are not simply didactic. In addition to pointing out the dangers of substance use, effective programs have lots of discussion, role-playing, and rehearsal of impulse-control skills. This means that successful programs require not only effective lessons, but skilled teachers to deliver them (Giles, et. al., 2010). (This may also explain why D.A.R.E.—which uses police officers as instructors—does poorly when objectively evaluated.)

If your school has a substance-abuse pre-vention program, look it over to see if it meets these basic requirements for effectiveness. Above all, advocate for substance awareness to be just one part of a comprehensive approach to social and emotional learning. Remember, it's much easier for a stressed, impressionable young teen to "just say no" when they are also developing the capacity to say "yes" to healthy alternatives to drugs and alcohol.

Social & Emotional Learning by Tom Conklin © 2014 Scholastic Teaching Resources

Resilience

"So Matilda's strong young mind continued to grow, nurtured by the voices
of all those authors who had sent their books out into the world like ships
on the sea. These books gave Matilda a hopeful and comforting message:
You are not alone."

FROM *Matilda*, BY ROALD DAHL

Cliques. Bullies. Aggression. Depression. Addiction.
Enough already!
When tackling the social and emotional lives of middle schools students, it's all
too easy to get bogged down in addressing the troubles that many young teens face, and
to ignore the amazing strengths and abilities shown by youngsters as they transition
to their teen years. If it's true that middle school can be a challenging and stressful
period in anyone's life, it's also true that being exposed to the strains of middle school
gives youngsters the opportunity to identify and develop their strengths, all as part of
their journey of self-discovery. To put it another way, middle school is the place where
resiliency can truly blossom.

Think of the word *resilient*, and what comes to mind? A sturdy rubber ball that
will always bounce back; a hardy little pup that won't take no for an answer when he
wants some lap time; a scrappy underdog team that will never admit defeat. Resilient
is the word to describe anyone or anything that will stay true to itself and will not
quit, no matter what. Resiliency is also a term used by psychologists to describe the
combination of personal traits and external relationships that determine how well
an individual handles adversity. Let's sum up our exploration of social and emotional
learning with a look at resiliency.

The clinical definition of psychological resilience describes it as "the process of
overcoming the negative effects of risk exposure, coping successfully with traumatic
experiences, and avoiding the negative trajectories associated with risks" (Fergus &
Zimmerman, 2005). Note the definition of resilience as a *process*, not as a descriptive
trait or a personal quality. Resilience is a description of what a person does, not who
they are. Since it is a process, not an inherent trait, resilience can be nurtured and
developed, just like artistic or athletic talent. There are two broad dimensions to
psychological resilience, and each deserves attention as you try to help young teens
develop the ability to overcome risk and hardships and maximize their ability to
bounce back.

The first dimension of psychological resilience, *resources*, refers to the external
relationships (parents, teachers, peers) that lend support and provide guidance to the
teen. Think of resources as the "social" dimension in social emotional learning. The
second dimension of resilience is called *assets*, and refers to the individual teen's inner

strengths, including "competence, coping skills, and self-efficacy" (ibid.). Think of these inner assets as the "emotional" dimension in social and emotional learning. Seen this way, the end result of social and emotional learning will be resiliency.

Matilda, the young heroine of Roald Dahl's darkly funny novel, is a model of resiliency. Matilda has plenty of psychological assets: intelligence, patience, and kindness. (She also has telekinetic powers—but that's a different class of asset!) Despite having grotesquely awful parents and a sadistic school headmistress in Miss Trunchbull, Matilda also has social resources: a set of friends and Miss Honey, her kind and sympathetic teacher. As her story unfolds, Matilda has a positive effect on her environment and relationships, especially by forming a deep bond with Miss Honey, whose fortune Matilda restores and who ultimately adopts Matilda.

Perhaps Matilda's most significant resource for resilience is her love of literature. The quote from the book that opens this chapter captures the essence of literature in the social and emotional learning context. A great book holds a mirror up to the reader and shows her what she is, or what she may become. *To Kill a Mockingbird, The Outsiders, The Adventures of Huckleberry Finn*—these and other classics of young adult fiction present young readers with the chance to confront and work through the most difficult personal and moral issues. Most important, the heroes of great fiction prove to the young reader—like Matilda—that he or she is not alone. Placing one's own experiences into the broader context of human experience is one of the great rewards of reading literature, and it's also a necessary part of the resiliency process.

Our final activity will call upon your students' favorite literary characters to help them identify the qualities of resilience, and to help them see that, no matter what challenges we face, no one is truly alone.

LESSON 20

I Can Identify . . .

SEL Objectives: 1, 2, 4, 8, 9

Preparing the Lesson
Make copies of Worksheet 25: I Can Identify . . . (page 125).

Warm Up
Ask students with whom they identify. Tell them that they could mention celebrities, athletes, peers, family members—anybody they identify with. As students share their answers, have them say why they identify with that individual. Do they share common attitudes? Experiences? Interests? Have one or two students define in their own words what it means to identify with someone.

Using the Lesson

1. Continue the Warm Up activity, but expand it to include fictional characters. With which characters in books or movies do students identify? After students have chosen characters, focus the discussion on the personal qualities of those characters (e.g., courage, a sense of humor, common interests or fears) that students identify with. As students name those personal qualities, list them on the board.

2. Next, extend the discussion to include the situations that the characters are in that make them "relatable." Do the characters have relationships like those in the students' lives? Do they have similar friends, rivals, family members? If some students cite characters from fantasy or science fiction, ask students if even those characters have relationships that people in real life can relate to. (For instance, Frodo in *Lord of the Rings* has a devoted friend in Sam and an older mentor in Gandalf. Students in real life have similar relationships.)

3. Finally, ask students if they face similar challenges as their favorite characters. These connections will be self-evident in realistic works of fiction. Fantasies may present a more difficult and abstract connection for students to make. For instance, in *The Hunger Games*, Katniss's dilemma as a participant in the games is far beyond anything a teen will face in real life. However, elicit from fans of the story if they have ever felt pressure to perform well in athletics or a school performance or risk letting people down. Discuss how good fantasy stories take common dilemmas people face and blow them up into bigger, more exciting versions in fantastic settings.

4. Distribute Worksheet 25 and have students fill in the lists of personal qualities and relationships for three characters with whom they identify. Tell them to focus on positive qualities and helpful relationships.

5. After completing the lists for fictional characters, tell students to put their own name in the last space. Challenge them to pick qualities they have identified in the fictional characters that they themselves possess. Have them write those qualities below their names, and list people they can rely on in the relationships column.

6. After they have filled in their worksheets, let volunteers share which of their characters they identify with most, and why, citing as evidence the personal qualities and relationships they have in common.

Wrap Up

End the lesson by asking students why they admire the characters they have analyzed. Point out that the reasons we admire someone can be different from the reasons we like someone—for example, you can like someone because they are friendly, but you would admire them for being friendly to people who are different or outcasts.

Odds are that in the cases of most main characters in young adult fiction, a primary reason for admiring them will be something along the lines of "they overcame adversity" or "they didn't give up." When students mention those sorts of admirable qualities, introduce the word *resilience* and write it on the board. Ask students to define resilience in their own words ("you bounce back" or "you keep on trying"). Talk about what makes their favorite characters resilient. Elicit that each character's personal qualities and supportive relationships are factors that make the characters able to bounce back. Ask students if they are resilient and what makes them that way.

Extending the Lesson

Have students create "fan fiction" starring their favorite characters and including themselves, the students, as characters in the story. How would they get along with their favorite characters? Would they be alike? Different? What sorts of conflicts would they have? What challenges might they face or overcome?

Social & Emotional Learning © 2014 by Tom Conklin, Scholastic Teaching Resources

Name _____ Date _____

What Are My Traits?

You may have chosen from a list of traits like this when you made characters for a video game. This is no game! Which of these traits describe you? Which traits would you like to have in the future? Mark the traits you have and those you want to have.

Have	Want to Have		Have	Want to Have	
❑	❑	Absent-Minded	❑	❑	Grumpy
❑	❑	Adventurous	❑	❑	Handy
❑	❑	Artistic	❑	❑	Heavy Sleeper
❑	❑	Athletic	❑	❑	Hot-Headed
❑	❑	Bookworm	❑	❑	Light Sleeper
❑	❑	Born Salesperson	❑	❑	Loner
❑	❑	Brave	❑	❑	Loves the Cold
❑	❑	Brooding	❑	❑	Loves the Heat
❑	❑	Cat Person	❑	❑	Loves the Outdoors
❑	❑	Clumsy	❑	❑	Mooch
❑	❑	Computer Whiz	❑	❑	Neat
❑	❑	Couch Potato	❑	❑	Night Owl
❑	❑	Coward	❑	❑	Nurturing
❑	❑	Daredevil	❑	❑	Perceptive
❑	❑	Disciplined	❑	❑	Perfectionist
❑	❑	Diva	❑	❑	Proper
❑	❑	Dog Person	❑	❑	Rebellious
❑	❑	Dramatic	❑	❑	Schmoozer
❑	❑	Eco-Friendly	❑	❑	Shy
❑	❑	Excitable	❑	❑	Slob
❑	❑	Family-Oriented	❑	❑	Social Butterfly
❑	❑	Friendly	❑	❑	Unlucky
❑	❑	Frugal	❑	❑	Vegetarian
❑	❑	Good Sense of Humor	❑	❑	Workaholic

Name _____ Date _____

Introvert or Extravert?

TRUE or FALSE

Write T (True) or F (False) next to the following statements.

____ **1.** Some people might say I'm boring.

____ **2.** If you have a problem with me, tell me to my face.

____ **3.** I work well as part of a team.

____ **4.** I speak before I think.

____ **5.** People tire me out.

____ **6.** I almost never pick up when my cell phone rings.

____ **7.** I make people laugh.

____ **8.** I can text, play a video game, and help my brother with his homework—at the same time.

____ **9.** My dream weekend? Just kicking back, with nothing at all to do.

____ **10.** I'd rather hang out with one friend than go to the mall with a group.

____ **11.** I hate it when people look over my shoulder when I'm doing something.

____ **12.** I hate writing in a journal.

____ **13.** I hate to be alone.

____ **14.** I am going to be rich and famous. Seriously.

____ **15.** I don't say much unless I really know you.

____ **16.** I'm a good listener.

____ **17.** When it's my birthday, please don't make a big deal out if it.

____ **18.** I really, really do not like homework.

____ **19.** I focus on one task at a time.

____ **20.** I'm a thrill-seeker.

HOW TO SCORE THE SURVEY

• Give yourself 1 point each time you answered True for:
2, 3, 4, 7, 8, 12, 13, 14, 18, 20. Add up those points. This is your *E* score.

E = _____

• Next, give yourself 1 point each time you answered True for:
1, 5, 6, 9, 10, 11, 15, 16, 17, 19. Add up those points. This is your *I* score.

I = _____

• Subtract your *I* score from your *E* score. *(The answer may be a negative number.)* Then circle your answer on the number line below:

_____

Introvert   Ambivert   Extravert

-10 -9 -8 -7 -6 -5 -4 -3 -2 -1 0 1 2 3 4 5 6 7 8 9 10

ARE YOU AN INTROVERT?

You are energized by being alone.
You think before you speak.
You put up with social situations.
You like to think things through.

Being an introvert is NOT necessarily the same as being "shy."

ARE YOU AN EXTRAVERT?

You are energized by other people.
You "shoot from the hip."
You enjoy social situations.
You like to talk things out.

Being an extravert is NOT necessarily the same as being "hyper."

WORKSHEET • 3

Optimist or Pessimist?

Read each statement. Circle the number that reflects how well the statement describes you.

		No way!			That's me!
1. Things usually turn out for the best for me.		1	2	3	4
2. It's easy for me to relax.		1	2	3	4
3. If something can go wrong, it will!		1	2	3	4
4. My future's so bright, I've got to wear shades.		1	2	3	4
5. I enjoy my friends a lot.		1	2	3	4
6. I always keep busy.		1	2	3	4
7. I hardly ever count on things going my way.		1	2	3	4
8. It doesn't take much to get me angry.		1	2	3	4
9. I do not get my hopes up.		1	2	3	4
10. When all is said and done, I expect more good things to happen to me than bad things to happen.		1	2	3	4

HOW TO SCORE THE SURVEY

• Cross out questions 2, 5, 6, and 8. They are fillers.

• Add up the answers to questions 1, 4, and 10. This is your O score.   O = _____

• Add up the answers to questions 3, 7, and 9. This is your P score.   P = _____

• Subtract your P score from your O score. *(The answer may be a negative number.)* Then circle your answer on the number line below: _____

Pessimist   Optimist

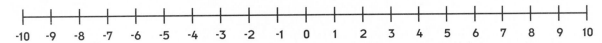

-10 -9 -8 -7 -6 -5 -4 -3 -2 -1 0 1 2 3 4 5 6 7 8 9 10

WHAT'S YOUR ATTITUDE? _____

Feelings

PRIMARY EMOTIONS

Joy	Sadness	Trust	Disgust
Fear	Anger	Surprise	Anticipation

COMPLEX FEELINGS

Surprise
+ Fear
_____
Alarm

Disgust
+ Anticipation
_____
Cynicism

Sadness
+ Anticipation
_____
Pessimism

Anticipation
+ Anger
_____
Aggression

Sadness
+ Fear
_____
Guilt

Joy
+ Anger
_____
Pride

Fear
+ Anticipation
_____
Anxiety

Joy
+ Trust
_____
Love

Surprise
+ Anger
_____
Rage

Surprise
+ Trust
_____
Curiosity

Joy
+ Anticipation
_____
Optimism

Disgust
+ Fear
_____
Shame

Can you "add up" two primary emotions so that they equal another feeling?
Write a paragraph explaining how the emotions "add up."

_____   _____

_____   + _____

_____   _____

_____

Brain Freezers

How fast can you answer these riddles?

---

1. A video game console and one video game together cost $110. The game console costs $100 more than the video game. How much does the video game cost?

5. A horse meets a priest, who then disappears. Where does this take place?

---

2. It takes 5 machines 5 minutes to make 5 widgets. How long does it take 100 machines to make 100 widgets?

6. What is one common question that you can never honestly answer "yes"?

---

3. How many of each type of animal did Moses take on the ark?

7. A police officer saw a truck driver going the wrong way down a one-way street. The officer did nothing when he saw this. Why not?

---

4. Your mother has three children: April, May, and . . . what's the third child's name?

8. A man is pushing his car and stops in front of a hotel. He then realizes that he is bankrupt. Why?

Circles of Myself

People I Know
About, but Who
Don't Know Me

People I Know
About, but Who
Don't Know Me

People I Hardly Know

My Outer Circle

My Inner Circle

Me

People I Know
About, but Who
Don't Know Me

Genograms

Use the male and female symbols to represent the people on your genogram. Use the other connecting symbols to show how the people get along with each other.

MARRIED

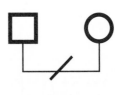

SEPARATED

DIVORCED

GETTING BACK TOGETHER AFTER DIVORCE

CLOSE

DISTANT

HOSTILE

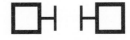

CUTOFF

Name _____ Date _____

Boundaries

Boundaries are rules that tell us what we can and can't do. There are three basic kinds of boundaries.

RIGID:

These are strict and do not change. You might not know why these rules are rules . . . but you do know that you have to follow them!

CLEAR:

You understand these rules. Clear boundaries can change, too. Some things that were "out of bounds" when you were younger might be okay now.

FUZZY:

These are "rules" that aren't really rules at all. A fuzzy boundary might be one that says that anything goes. Or it might be a rule that is strict one day, but totally ignored the next day.

Here are examples of boundaries. Write R (Rigid), C (Clear), or F (Fuzzy) next to each boundary.

____ "Beware of Dog!"

____ "You kids stay off my lawn!"

____ "Do unto others as you would have them do unto you."

____ "Mi casa es su casa."

____ "Your curfew is 9:00 p.m. sharp!"

____ "Good fences make good neighbors."

____ "This movie is rated PG-13. Parents are strongly cautioned. Some material may not be suitable for children under 13."

____ "I'm not going steady with anyone until high school, at the earliest."

____ "YOLO!" (You only live once.)

____ "You must be this tall to ride the roller coaster."

____ "The more the merrier!"

____ "Keep Out!"

____ "You can have the Internet password after you have done your homework and cleaned your room."

____ "Any friend of yours is a friend of mine."

What are your boundaries? _____

_____

Does your family have any boundaries? _____ Who sets them? _____

What kind of boundaries do you find most frustrating—rigid, clear, or fuzzy? Why? _____

_____

_____

_____

What Do Friends Do?

Friends . . .

Hang out.

Make each other laugh.
(And cry. And try new stuff.)

Have each other's back.

Make each other feel good about themselves.

Hold up a mirror to each other.

Share.
(Stuff. And thoughts. And feelings.)

What else do friends do?

Below write a brief autobiographical essay. Describe a friendship you have with a classmate. Include examples of all the points listed above.

_____

_____

_____

_____

_____

_____

_____

_____

_____

_____

_____

Feel the Force

"The Force" is the power you have over other people, and the power other people have over you. These are the keys to mastering the Force:

- Knowing when you are influencing other people
- Knowing when other people are influencing you
- Using the Force for good . . . avoid the dark side!

The Good Side	POWERS OF THE FORCE	The Dark Side
ACCEPTANCE "I like you for who you are."	YOUR **FRIENDSHIP**	**REJECTION** "Do as I say, or I'm going to dump you."
ENCOURAGEMENT "You can do this! I believe in you!"	YOUR **OPINION**	**DISSING** "Only a LOSER would wear that hat."
MAKING A PLAN "If we both work at the car wash, we will have fun and raise money for a good cause."	YOUR **BRAIN**	**HATCHING A SCHEME** "No one will know if we copy our work off the Internet."

Come up with positive and negative examples of the Force in action. Write a short skit using one of these situations:

You and your friends . . .

- Prepare for a test
- Hang out at the mall
- Go to a school dance
- Meet a new student
- Put on a fundraiser

How Rude!

Here are examples of rude behavior, along with a list of emotions that cause people to act badly. Which emotion do you think causes each rude behavior?

EMOTIONS

ANGER:
"Grrrrrr."

ARROGANCE:
"I'm better than you."

ATTITUDE:
"You got a problem with me?"

SELFISHNESS:
"I want what I want."

VANITY: "Look at me! Look at me!"

On the School Bus

BEHAVIOR	EMOTION
Making fun of the driver.	_____
Throwing spit wads.	_____
Pulling the emergency brake when there is no emergency.	_____

At the Movies

BEHAVIOR	EMOTION
Texting.	_____
Talking to your friends.	_____
Kicking the seat in front of you.	_____

At School

BEHAVIOR	EMOTION
Laughing at people behind their back.	_____
Putting gum under a desk.	_____
Dropping trash on the floor.	_____

In the Lunchroom

BEHAVIOR	EMOTION
Cutting in line.	_____
Telling a new girl that she can't sit with you.	_____
Knocking over someone's tray.	_____

At a Family Dinner

BEHAVIOR	EMOTION
Eating with your mouth wide open.	_____
Yawning when a sibling is talking.	_____
Storming from the table when your mom asks you to stop yawning and chew with your mouth closed.	_____

At a Sports Event

BEHAVIOR	EMOTION
Screaming at the other team's coach.	_____
Jumping over the fence and running across the field.	_____
Laughing hysterically when a player makes a mistake.	_____

WORKSHEET • 12

What Sets You Off?

Think of times that you have been angry. Really, *really* angry. Fill in the blanks for each anger incident you remember well.

WHERE did it happen? _____   WHEN did it happen? _____

WHO made you angry? _____

WHAT did that person do to set you off? _____

_____

HOW did you display your anger? _____

_____

WHERE did it happen? _____   WHEN did it happen? _____

WHO made you angry? _____

WHAT did that person do to set you off? _____

_____

HOW did you display your anger? _____

_____

WHERE did it happen? _____   WHEN did it happen? _____

WHO made you angry? _____

WHAT did that person do to set you off? _____

_____

HOW did you display your anger? _____

_____

Do you see a pattern? How can you change the pattern? _____

_____

_____

_____

Chill

You can't control other people. Sometimes they make you angry.
But you *can* control how you act when you get angry.

When someone gets you angry . . .

Take space.

Remove yourself from the situation, if you can.

Count to ten.

Or 100, if you need to. Counting does two things. It buys you time, and distracts you from whatever is setting you off.

Breathe deep.

Take a deep breath with every number that you count. When you breathe deep, your brain tells your body to calm down. Your heart rate slows down and your muscles relax.

Don't react! *Respond.*

Before you say anything, ask yourself: "Will this make matters better, or worse?" Here's a trick: Use "I" statements.

> Instead of saying, "You tick me off!"
> Say this: "I feel upset when you do that."

When you focus on yourself and your feelings, the other person will not feel under attack. That can help defuse the situation.

If all else fails, WALK AWAY.

Making a Scene

There's no secret to improving your improv. Just follow these guidelines:

1. Pay attention.
Be in the moment, and pay attention to what other people say and do.

2. Think about what is going on.
Watch the other people in the scene, and figure out why they do what they do.

3. Have a goal.
What does your character want out of the scene? Come up with a realistic goal.

4. Keep an open mind.
Don't get stuck in a rut. Come up with unique ways to respond to the other people in your scene. Here's a hint: Never say "no."

5. Be open to options.
How do you decide what to do next as the scene unfolds? If you pay attention to and interact with other people, you may figure out new and interesting ways to achieve your goal, or you might even set a better goal.

6. Go for it.
Make your scene!

I've Seen This One Before

We all have drama in our lives. Some "dramas" we rerun over and over and over again. What drama do you keep repeating?

Title:
Main characters:
What starts it off:
How it builds (and builds, and builds!):
How it (usually) ends:
How it can change:

Emojis

How are you feeling? Say it with an emoji! Draw facial expressions and stick figures to show body language. Start with the feelings here, then come up with your own on another sheet of paper.

Afraid	Annoyed	Apprehensive
Angry	Bored	Determined
Disgusted	Ecstatic	Happy
Interested	Joyful	Pensive
Sad	Surprised	Terrorized
Tired	Trusting	Vengeful

Nonverbal Scorecard

Describe in detail at least one example of each type of nonverbal communication. Identify the mood or feeling being communicated.

Facial Expression	Body Language
Personal Space	Eye Gaze
Touch	Appearance

What's Their Attitude? (Part I)

There are four types of attitude when it comes to interacting with people.

Aggressive

Motto: "I want what I want when I want it!"

Description: Stands up for himself or herself and doesn't care who gets hurt in the process.

Passive

Motto: "Peace and quiet."

Description: Does anything to avoid a conflict.

Passive-Aggressive

Motto: "Whatever."

Description: Secretly angry. Can be aggressive, but will deny it.

Assertive

Motto: "Live and let live."

Description: Stands up for himself or herself and respects other people, too.

Here are descriptions of four characters from *The Outsiders* by S.E. Hinton. Identify each one as AG (Aggressive), P (Passive), PA (Passive-Aggressive), or AS (Assertive).

_____ **Ponyboy**

Gets good grades. Runs track. Won't start a fight, but won't run away. Says what he thinks, and listens to others.

_____ **Cherry**

A popular girl who acts cool and aloof. Flirts with boys that her boyfriend doesn't like.

_____ **Dally**

Fights a lot. People fear him and treat him with respect. Goes out of his way to confront his enemies.

_____ **Johnny**

Very nervous and jumpy, is very shy with strangers. Often targeted by bullies.

What's Their Attitude? (Part II)

Here are excerpts from the novel *The Outsiders* by S.E. Hinton. What type of attitude does each one show? Identify each as aggressive, passive, passive-aggressive, or assertive. Then explain why.

1. *Ponyboy talks to Cherry:* "Do you think that your spying for us makes up for the fact that you're sitting there in a Corvette while my brother drops out of high school to get a job? Don't you ever try to give us handouts and then feel high and mighty about it." (Chapter 8, pp. 98–99)

   _____

   _____

2. *Ponyboy responds to threats from a group of Socs:* "'You know what a Soc is?' I said, my voice trembling with rage. 'White trash with Mustangs and madras.' And then, because I couldn't think of anything bad enough to call them, I spit at them." (Chapter 4, p. 43)

   _____

   _____

3. *Ponyboy thinks about why his friends get into fights:* "Soda fought for fun, Darry for pride, and Two-Bit for conformity. Why do I fight? I thought, and couldn't think of any real good reason. There isn't any real good reason for fighting except self-defense." (Chapter 9, p. 104)

   _____

   _____

4. *Cherry explains why she is different from Ponyboy and his friends:* "It's not just money. You greasers have a different set of values. You're more emotional. We're sophisticated—cool to the point of not feeling anything. Nothing is real for us." (Chapter 3, p. 30)

   _____

   _____

5. *Ponyboy talks about loyalty:* "You stick up for your buddies, no matter what they do. When you're a gang, you stick up for the members. If you don't stick up for them, stick together, make like brothers, it isn't a gang anymore. It's a pack. A snarling, distrustful, bickering pack." (Chapter 2, p. 22)

   _____

   _____

Conflict Resolution (Part I)

Everyone gets into conflicts. It happens when you want something, and another person wants something else. How well can you resolve a conflict? Your attitude has a lot to do with it.

Here are four types of attitudes and how they each resolve conflicts.

Aggressive

I WIN/YOU LOSE

Never give in.

It's not enough that you win, the other person has to lose.

Passive

YOU WIN/I LOSE

Always give in.

To keep the peace, you ignore your own needs.

Passive-Aggressive

I LOSE/YOU LOSE

Usually give in, but figure out a way to sabotage the other person.

You don't really care if you win, as long as the other person loses, too.

Assertive

I WIN/YOU WIN

Compromise in order to get most of what you want.

You stand up for yourself, but you want the other person to be satisfied, too.

A. Which of these attitudes is best for resolving conflicts so that they stay resolved? Why?

_____

_____

B. Which of these attitudes is the hardest to deal with? Why?

_____

_____

C. Which attitude is the hardest one to keep if you are in a conflict? Why?

_____

_____

Conflict Resolution (Part II)

Here are some typical conflicts people have. See if you can find a win/win solution for each one. Write your solution or jot down some notes on this page.

1. George has been playing a video game for ten minutes and is in the middle of a challenging level. Ashley comes in and says that she has to leave for the dentist in a half hour. She's nervous and wants to relax by playing a dance game on the game system.

_____

_____

2. Kelly is studying for a huge set of tests later in the week. Her little sister has the bedroom next to hers and is listening to annoying music at top volume on her stereo.

_____

_____

3. Morgan's daily chore is to do the dishes after dinner each night. She just learned that she has a part in the school play and will have to rehearse at night, right after dinner. Morgan's mother works hard all day and is too tired to do the dishes. Morgan really wants to be in the school play.

_____

_____

4. Jenesis spends the hours after school at the library because her mother works. Some older girls from Jenesis's school hang out outside the library smoking cigarettes. When Jenesis refuses to join them, they begin to tease her. Jenesis doesn't want to go to the library anymore because of them, but her mom wants her to stay there, since the library is a safe place.

_____

_____

5. Austin's best friend, Pete, is going through a hard time. His parents have split up, and Pete has been doing poorly in school. He was suspended twice for acting up in class. Austin wants to be there for his friend and asks his parents for permission to have Pete come to their house for a sleepover. Austin's mom is okay with the plan, but his dad refuses, saying that Pete is a bad influence.

_____

_____

Bullying Survey

STUDENTS

Please answer the following questions.

1. Have you been the victim of bullying, or witnessed another student
    being bullied, at any time within the past 12 months?   YES / NO

    If "yes," how many bullying incidents have you witnessed or been the victim of?

    a. 1–2   b. 3–5   c. More than 5

2. If you have been bullied, what did the bullies do to you?

    a. Teased and/or made threats

    b. Started rumors about me or made me feel left out

    c. Pushed me, hit me, spit on me, or physically hurt me some other way

3. If you were bullied, what did you do? Rate how well this helped solve the bullying problem on a
    scale of 1–5, with 1 being "no help at all" and 5 being "a big help."

a. Walked away	1	2	3	4	5
b. Fought back	1	2	3	4	5
c. Told a friend	1	2	3	4	5
d. Told an adult at school	1	2	3	4	5
e. Told an adult at home	1	2	3	4	5

4. If you were bullied and told an adult about it, what did that adult do? Rate how well this helped
    solve the bullying problem on a scale of 1–5, with 1 being "no help at all" and 5 being "a big help."

a. Listened to me	1	2	3	4	5
b. Punished the bully	1	2	3	4	5
c. Told me to fight my own battles	1	2	3	4	5
d. Told me to avoid the bully	1	2	3	4	5
e. Asked me later how I was doing	1	2	3	4	5

5. How would you rate bullying as a problem at your school?

    a. Not a problem

    b. A problem, but not too bad

    c. A problem

    d. A very serious problem

Bullying Survey

PARENTS

Please answer the following questions.

1. Have you heard of any bullying incidents in our school within the
   past 12 months?   YES / NO

   If "yes," how many bullying incidents have you heard about?

   a. 1–2

   b. 3–5

   c. More than 5

2. If one or more students told you that he or she had been bullied, what did you do?

   a. Listened to the victims

   b. Reported it to the school

   c. Told the victims to fight their own battles

   d. Told the victims to avoid the bully

   e. Followed up with the victims later to see how they were doing

3. How would you rate bullying as a problem at your child's school?

   a. Not a problem

   b. A problem, but not too bad

   c. A problem

   d. A very serious problem

Bullying Survey

SCHOOL PERSONNEL

Please answer the following questions.

1. Have you witnessed or heard of any bullying incidents in our school
   within the past 12 months?   YES / NO

   If "yes," how many bullying incidents have you heard about?

   a. 1–2

   b. 3–5

   c. More than 5

2. If one or more students told you that he or she had been bullied, what did you do?

   a. Listened to the victims

   b. Punished the bully

   c. Told the victims to fight their own battles

   d. Told the victims to avoid the bully

   e. Followed up with the victims later to see how they were doing

3. How would you rate bullying as a problem at your school?

   a. Not a problem

   b. A problem, but not too bad

   c. A problem

   d. A very serious problem

Self-Spin

"Spin" is what you call it when you try to talk someone into seeing things your way. Sometimes we "spin" ourselves—and we don't even realize it! Here are nine types of self-spin. Spin yourself with one of these, and it can stress you out.

1. Black-and-White Thinking
When you are sure that things are all good or all bad, with no middle ground.

2. Blanket Thoughts
When you think that a single bad event means that nothing good will ever happen again. (Blanket thoughts can smother you!)

3. Tunnel Vision
You focus on the negative so much you can't see anything positive.

4. Mind Reading
You think you know what other people think and don't bother finding out if you are right.

5. Misfortune Telling
You always predict that things will go wrong.

6. Catastrophizing
You believe that every little thing that goes wrong is a huge disaster.

7. Shoulds/Oughts/Musts
You think things should be a certain way—and get upset when life doesn't go the way you think it should.

8. Label-Making
You label people and things, even yourself. For instance, if you flunk a test, you label yourself "stupid" instead of thinking "I should have studied more."

9. Woe Is Me
When bad things happen, you think it's all because of you, not just bad luck.

Need a Coping Skill? It's as Easy as A-B-C

We all have problems that can cause us to stress out. Here's an A-B-C model that shows how we get stressed.

A	B	C
stands for ADVERSITY you face	stands for your BELIEF about it	stands for CONSEQUENCES
Example: **BIG MATH TEST**	*Example:* **"I'LL NEVER PASS!"**	*Example:* **STRESS/PANIC/"F"**

If you want to change C, first you have to change A or B. You usually can't control adversity, but you *can* control what you believe about it.

A	B	C
stands for ADVERSITY you face	stands for your BELIEF about it	stands for CONSEQUENCES
Example: **BIG MATH TEST**	*Example:* ~~"I'LL NEVER PASS!"~~	*Example:* ~~STRESS/PANIC/"F"~~
	"I'VE GOT THIS! I CAN DO IT!"	**CHILL/STUDY/"A"**

Fill in some A-B-C's of your own. Think of an adversity you face, what you believe about the adversity and how you can handle it, and the consequences.

A	B	C
stands for ADVERSITY you face	stands for your BELIEF about it	stands for CONSEQUENCES
_____	_____	_____
_____	_____	_____

A	B	C
stands for ADVERSITY you face	stands for your BELIEF about it	stands for CONSEQUENCES
_____	_____	_____
_____	_____	_____

I Can Identify . . .

Think of your favorite fictional characters. What makes them so special? Write the names of three favorite characters in the slots below. Then fill in the lists. The first list should include their best personal qualities (like a sense of humor or bravery). The second list should include all of the other characters they know and rely on. When you've made lists for three characters, do a fourth one for a very important character: you!

CHARACTER: _____

QUALITIES   RELATIONSHIPS

_____   _____

_____   _____

_____   _____

_____   _____

CHARACTER: _____

QUALITIES   RELATIONSHIPS

_____   _____

_____   _____

_____   _____

_____   _____

CHARACTER: _____

QUALITIES   RELATIONSHIPS

_____   _____

_____   _____

_____   _____

_____   _____

YOUR NAME: _____

QUALITIES   RELATIONSHIPS

_____   _____

_____   _____

_____   _____

_____   _____

What personal qualities do you have in common with your favorite characters? What are your most important relationships?

_____

_____

Which character do you identify with the most? Why?

_____

_____

References

American Psychiatric Association. (2013). *Diagnostic and statistical manual of mental disorders (5th ed.). DSM-5.* Washington, D.C.: American Psychiatric Publishing.

American Psychological Association. *Suicide warning signs.* Retrieved from http://www.apa.org/topics/suicide/signs.aspx

Balsa, A.I., Homer, J.F., French, M.T., & Norton, E.C. (2010). Alcohol use and popularity: Social payoffs from conforming to peers' behavior. *Journal of Research on Adolescence, 21*(3), 559–568.

Battistella, E.L. (2009). The yardstick of manners. *Culture and Society, 46*(4), 363–367.

Baumeister, R.F., Campbell, J.D., Krueger, J.I., & Vohs, K.D. (2003). Does high self-esteem cause better performance, interpersonal happiness, or healthier lifestyles? *Psychological Science in the Public Interest, 4*(1), 1–44.

Bazelon, E. (2013). *Sticks and stones: Defeating the culture of bullying and rediscovering the power of character and empathy.* New York: Random House.

Bronfenbrenner, U. (1994). *Ecological models of human development.* International Encyclopedia of Education, Vol. 3. (2nd ed.). Oxford: Elsevier. Reprinted in: Gauvain, M. & Cole. M. (Eds.). *Readings on the development of children.* (2nd ed.). (1993). New York: Freeman.

Buhrmester, D., & Furman, W. (1987). The development of companionship and intimacy. *Child Development, 58*(4), 1101–1113.

Burns, D.D. (1980). *Feeling good: The new mood therapy.* New York: Harper Health.

Cain, S. (2011, January 27). Are you an introvert or extrovert and why does it matter? [Web log post]. Retrieved from http://www.thepowerofintroverts.com/2011/01/27/quiz-are-you-an-introvert-or-an-extrovert-and-why-does-it-matter/

Cain, S. (2012). *Quiet: The power of introverts in a world that can't stop talking.* New York: Broadway Books.

Carver, C.S. (2007) LOT-R (Life orientation test-revised) [Web post]. Retrieved from http://www.psy.miami.edu/faculty/ccarver/CCscales.html

Coie, J.D., Dodge, K.A., & Coppotelli, H. (1982). Dimensions and types of social status: A cross-age perspective. *Developmental Psychology, 18*(4), 557–570.

Costandi, M. (2013). *50 human brain ideas you really need to know.* London: Quercus.

Crick N.R., & Dodge, K.A. (1994). A review and reformulation of social information-processing mechanisms in children's social adjustment. *Psychological Bulletin, 115*(1), 74–101.

Csikszentmihalyi, M. (2009). *Flow.* New York: HarperCollins.

Davis, S. (2009, September/October). The truth about bullying. *Psychotherapy Networker,* 19–21.

Dunbar, R. (2010, December 25). You've got to have (150) friends. [Electronic version]. *New York Times.*

Durlak, J.A., Weissberg R.P., Dymnicki, A.B., Taylor, R.D., & Schellinger, K.B. (2011). The impact of enhancing students' social and emotional learning: A meta-analysis of school-based universal interventions. *Child Development, 82*(1), 405–432.

Ellis, A., & Harper R.A. (1997). *A guide to rational living.* Chatsworth, CA: Wilshire Book Co.

Erikson, E. (1959, 1980). *Identity and the Life Cycle,* New York: W.W. Norton & Co.

Fergus, S., & Zimmerman, M.A. (2005). Adolescent resilience: A framework for understanding healthy development in the face of risk. *Annual Review of Public Health 2005, 26,* 399–419.

Fuligni, A.J., Barber, B.L., Eccles, J.S., & Clements, P. (2001). Early adolescent peer orientation and adjustment during high school. *Developmental Psychology, 37*(1), 28–36.

Furnham, A., Chamorro-Premuzic, T., & McDougall, F. (2003). Personality, cognitive ability, and beliefs about intelligence as predictors of academic performance. *Learning and Individual Differences, 14,* 49–66.

Gasser, L., & Keller, M. (2009). Are the competent the morally good? Perspective taking and moral motivation of children involved in bullying. *Social Development, 18*(4), 798–816.

Giles, S., Pankratz, M.M., Ringwalt, C., Hansen, W.B., Dusenbury, L., & Jackson-Newsom, J. (2010). Teachers' delivery skills and substance abuse prevention program outcome: The moderating role of students' need for cognition and impulse decision making. *Journal of Drug Education, 40*(4), 395–410.

Goleman, D. (1995). *Emotional intelligence.* New York: Bantam Books.

Henrich, C.H., Kuperminc, G.P., Sack, A., Blatt, S.J., & Leadbeater, B.J. (2000). Characteristics and homogeneity of early adolescent friendship groups: A comparison of male and female clique and nonclique members. *Applied Developmental Science, 4*(1), 15–26.

Hill, N.E., & Tyson, D.F. (2009). Parental involvement in middle school: A meta-analytic assessment of the strategies that promote achievement. *Developmental Psychology, 45*(3), 740–763.

Hobson, L.B. (2004, April 24). Weekend warrior [online entertainment news post]. Retrieved from http://jam.canoe.ca/Television/TV_Shows/S/Saturday_Night_Live/2004/04/28/pf-733201.html

How do you do? http://www.youtube.com/watch?v=eiD91wPLQZA

Jackson, C., Geddes, R., Haw, S., & Frank, J. (2011). Interventions to prevent substance use and risky sexual behavior in young people: A systematic review. *Addiction Review,* (107), 733–747.

Jung, C.G. (1923). *Psychological types, or the psychology of individuation.* New York: Harcourt Brace.

Jung, C.G. (1936). Psychological typology. In Storr, A. (Ed.). (1983). *The essential Jung: Selected writings* Princeton: Princeton University Press.

Kahn, J. (2013, September 11). Can emotional intelligence be taught? *New York Times Magazine,* MM44.

Kahneman, D. (2011). *Thinking, fast and slow.* New York: Farrar, Straus and Giroux.

Kerbs, J.J., & Jolley, J.M. (2007). The joy of violence: What about violence is fun in middle-school? *American Journal of Criminal Justice, 32*(1–2), 12–29.

Kim, Y.S., & Leventhal B. (2008). Bullying and suicide. A review. *International Journal of Adolescent Medicine and Health, 20*(2), 133–154.

Kohlberg, L., & Hersh, R.H. (1977). Moral development: A review of the theory. *Theory into Practice, 16*(2), 53–59.

Kovacs, M. (1997). Depressive disorders in childhood: An impressionistic landscape. *Journal of Child Psychology and Psychiatry, 38*(3), 287–298. Cited by Freydenberg, E., et. al. (2004). Prevention is better than cure: Coping skills training for adolescents at school. *Educational Psychology in Practice, 20*(2), 117–134.

Krahe, B. Moller, I., Huesmann, L.R., Kirwil, L., Felber, J., & Berger, A. (2011). Desensitization to media violence: Links with habitual media violence exposure, aggressive cognitions, and aggressive behavior. *Journal of Personality and Social Psychology, 100*(4), 630–646.

Kunimatsu M.M., & Marsee, M. (2012). Examining the presence of anxiety in aggressive individuals: The illuminating role of fight-or-flight mechanisms. *Child Care Youth Forum, 41*(3), 247–258.

Larson, R.W., & Richards, M.H. (1994). Family emotions: Do young adolescents and their parents feel the same states? *Journal of Research on Adolescence, 4*(4), 567–583.

Lazarus, R.S. (1991). Progress on a cognitive-motivational-relational theory of emotion. *American Psychologist, 46*(8), 819–834.

Leventhal, A. (1994). Peer conformity during adolescence: An integration of developmental, situational, and individual characteristics. Paper presented at the meeting of the Society for Research on Adolescence, San Diego, February 1994.

Lochman J.E., Powell, N.R., Clanton, N., & McElroy, H.K. (2006). Chapter 9: Anger and aggression. In Bear G.G., & Minke, K.M. (Eds.). *Children's needs III: Development, prevention, and intervention.* Bethesda, MD: National Association of School Psychologists.

Markus, H., & Nurius, P. (1986). Possible selves. *American Psychologist, 41*(9), 954–969.

Martineau, H. (1837) *Society in America, vol.3.* London: Saunders and Otley. Reprinted in *Pediatrics, 65*(1), 138.

McGoldrick, M., & Gerson, R. (1986). *Genograms in family assessment.* New York: W.W. Norton & Co.

Mehrabian A., & Ferris, S.R. (1968). Inference of attitudes from nonverbal communication in two channels. *Journal of Consulting Psychology, 31*(3), 248–252.

Meier, A., & Allen, G. (2009). Romantic relationships from adolescence to young adulthood: Evidence from the National Longitudinal Study of Adolescent Health. *The Sociological Quarterly, 50*(2), 308–335.

Minuchin, S. (1974). *Families and family therapy.* Cambridge: Harvard University Press.

Minuchin, S. (1981). *Family therapy techniques.* Cambridge: Harvard University Press.

Nielsen Company. (2009). How teens use media: A Nielsen report on the myths and realities of teen media trends. Retrieved from http://www.nielsen.com/us/en/reports/2009/How-Teens-Use-Media.html

Olweus, D. (1995). Bullying or peer abuse at school: Facts and interventions. *Current Directions in Psychological Science, 4*(6), 196–200.

Olweus, D. (2011). Bullying at school and later criminality: Findings from three Swedish community samples. *Criminal Behavior and Mental Health, 21*(2), 151–156.

Pease A. (1981). *Body language.* London: Sheldon Press.

Peterson, C., & Seligman, M.E.P. (2004). *Character strengths and virtues: A handbook and classification.* American Psychological Association. New York: Oxford University Press.

Pew Research Center. (Issued Nov. 18, 2010). The decline of marriage and rise of new families. Retrieved from http://www.pewsocialtrends.org/2010/11/18/the-decline-of-marriage-and-rise-of-new-families/

Plutchik, R. (1991). *The emotions*. Lanham, MD: University Press of America.

Rideout, V.J., Foehr, U.G., & Roberts, D.F. (2010, January). Generation M2: Media in the lives of 8–18 year olds. Menlo Park, CA: Kaiser Foundation. Retrieved from http://kff.org/other/event/generation-m2-media-in-the-lives-of/

Rivers, I., & Noret, N. (2010). Participant roles in bullying behavior and their association with thoughts of ending one's life. *Crisis, 31*(3), 143–148.

Robers, S., Kemp, J., & Truman, J. (2013). *Indicators of school crime and safety: 2012* (NCES 2013-036/NCJ 241446). National Center for Education Statistics, U.S. Department of Education, and Bureau of Justice Statistics, Office of Justice Programs, U.S. Department of Justice. Washington, D.C.

Rogers, C.R. (1957). The necessary and sufficient conditions of therapeutic personality change. *Journal of Consulting Psychology, 21*(2), 95–103.

Rosenbaum, D.P. (2007). Just say no to D.A.R.E. *Criminology & Public Policy, 6*(4), 815–824.

Santrock, J. (2012). *A topical approach to life-span development (6th ed.)*. New York: McGraw-Hill.

Satir, V. (1972). *Peoplemaking*. Palo Alto, CA: Science and Behavior Books.

Seligman, M.E.P. (with Revich, K., Jaycox, L., & Gillham, J.) (1995). *The optimistic child*. New York: Houghton Mifflin Company.

Spoth, R., Trudeau, L., Shin, C., Ralston, E., Redmond, C., Greenberg, M., & Feinberg, M. (2013). Longitudinal effects of universal preventive intervention in prescription drug misuse: Three randomized controlled trials with late adolescents and young adults. *American Journal of Public Health, 103*(4), 665–672.

Stein, S.J., Mozdzierz, A.B., & Mozdzierz, G.J. (1998). The kinship of Adlerian family counseling and Minuchin's structural family therapy. *The Journal of Individual Psychology, 54*(1), 90–107.

Sullivan, H.S. (1953). *The interpersonal theory of psychiatry*. New York: W.W. Norton & Co.

Umberson, D., & Montez, J.K. (2010). Social relationships and health: A flashpoint for health policy. *Journal of Health and Social Behavior,* 2010; *51*(Suppl): S54–S66.

The National Center on Addiction and Substance Abuse at Columbia University. (2012, August). *National Survey of American Attitudes on Substance Abuse XVII: Teens*. Conducted by QEV Analytics, Ltd. Retrieved from http://www.casacolumbia.org/upload/2012/20120822teensurvey.pdf

Turner, J.S. *Encyclopedia of relationships across the lifespan*. (1996). Westport, CT: Greenwood Press.

U.S. Census Bureau. (Issued April 2012). Households and families, 2010. Retrieved from http://www.census.gov/prod/cen2010/briefs/c2010br-14.pdf

Vincus, A., Ringwalt, C., Harris, M.S., & Shamblen, S.R. (2010). A short-term, quasi-experimental evaluation of D.A.R.E.'s revised elementary school curriculum. *Journal of Drug Education, 40*(1), 37–49.

Wang, S. (2013, June 17). Peer pressure for teens paves the path to adulthood. Online *Wall Street Journal*. Retrieved from http://online.wsj.com/article/SB10001424127887324520904578551462766909232.html#printMode

Wentzel, K.R., & Asher, S.R. (1995). The academic lives of neglected, rejected, popular, and controversial children. *Child Development, 66*(3), 754–763.

Werner N.E., & Crick, N.R. (2004). Maladaptive peer relationships and the development of relational and physical aggression during middle childhood. *Social Development, 13*(4), 495–514.

Wise K., Bundy, K.A., Bundy, E.A., & Wise, L.A. (1991). Social skills training for young adolescents. *Adolescence, 26*(101), 233–241.

Wiseman, R. (2002). *Queen bees and wannabes*. New York: Crown Books.

Wright, P.H. (2000). As cited in Gale Group. (2002). *International encyclopedia of marriage and family*, the Gale Group, Macmillan Reference USA, 2000.

Young, J.E., Klosko, J.S., & Weishar, M.E. (2003). *Schema therapy—A practitioner's guide*. New York: The Guilford Press.